Contents

Introduction

THE RIGHTS OF CHILDREN is Volume 342 in the **ISSUES** series. The aim of the series is to offer current, diverse information about important issues in our world, from a UK perspective.

ABOUT THE RIGHTS OF CHILDREN

Children around the world are often engaged in paid and unpaid forms of work that are not harmful to them. However, they are classed as child labourers and when they are too young to work this can compromise their physical, mental, social or educational development. This book explores the rights of children throughout the world and the conditions in which some of those children are working. It also looks at child marriage and the steps being taken to try to combat this.

OUR SOURCES

Titles in the **ISSUES** series are designed to function as educational resource books, providing a balanced overview of a specific subject.

The information in our books is comprised of facts, articles and opinions from many different sources, including:

⇨ Newspaper reports and opinion pieces

⇨ Website factsheets

⇨ Magazine and journal articles

⇨ Statistics and surveys

⇨ Government reports

⇨ Literature from special interest groups.

A NOTE ON CRITICAL EVALUATION

Because the information reprinted here is from a number of different sources, readers should bear in mind the origin of the text and whether the source is likely to have a particular bias when presenting information (or when conducting their research). It is hoped that, as you read about the many aspects of the issues explored in this book, you will critically evaluate the information presented.

It is important that you decide whether you are being presented with facts or opinions. Does the writer give a biased or unbiased report? If an opinion is being expressed, do you agree with the writer? Is there potential bias to the 'facts' or statistics behind an article?

ASSIGNMENTS

In the back of this book, you will find a selection of assignments designed to help you engage with the articles you have been reading and to explore your own opinions. Some tasks will take longer than others and there is a mixture of design, writing and research-based activities that you can complete alone or in a group.

Useful weblinks

www.actionaid.org.uk

www.crae.org.uk

www.data.unicef.org

www.ethicaltrade.org

www.girlsnotbrides.org

www.ilo.org

www.independent.co.uk

www.inews.co.uk

www.ncb.org.uk

www.telegraph.co.uk

www.theconversation.com

www.theguardian.com

www.unicef.org.uk

www.worldbank.org

FURTHER RESEARCH

At the end of each article we have listed its source and a website that you can visit if you would like to conduct your own research. Please remember to critically evaluate any sources that you consult and consider whether the information you are viewing is accurate and unbiased.

State of children's rights in England 2017

An extract from Briefing 5: Immigration, Asylum & Trafficking

Introduction

The Government has committed to a number of positive steps in 2017 to improve practice and policy to safeguard unaccompanied children, given the increase in numbers. However, longstanding concerns of the UN Committee have still not been addressed in relation to age assessments, child detention and the treatment of undocumented children. Family reunification for children both coming to, and already in, the UK was a key issue raised by the Human Rights Council in this year's UPR and remains an ongoing concern. The UK's forthcoming exit from the EU also raises worrying questions for children of European nationals living in the UK.

Where do we need to improve?

Immigration and asylum

No durable solution for unaccompanied children

After a large increase in 2015, the numbers of unaccompanied children seeking asylum in the UK have remained high but stable: 3,290 in 2016 – a 1% increase on the previous year.

In 2016, there were significant increases in the number of children seeking asylum from Iran, Iraq and Sudan. Only 30% of unaccompanied children were granted refugee status in 2016. Although this is a small increase compared to last year (22%), the majority (50%) were still refused asylum and were granted a temporary form of leave (UASC leave), compared to 52% in 2015. Such temporary leave is rarely in children's best interests as it does not provide them with a durable solution.

Applications from Afghanistan increased in 2015 and 2016 after several years of decreasing. As table 1 on page 3 shows, there is great variation in asylum acceptance rates between nationalities. Albania is the country with the highest refusal rate. Compared with pre-2015 figures, there was a large reduction in the number of applicants from Eritrea who were granted refugee status, from 95% to 44%.

Ongoing concerns about National Transfer Scheme

The National Transfer Scheme (NTS), a new voluntary transfer arrangement between local authorities for unaccompanied asylum-seeking children, has now been operating for over a year. However concerns are still being raised including: delays in transferring children, lack of best interest assessments, delays in access to vital statutory services, poor communication with children and foster carers, lack of clarity on age assessments, and confusion over the continued voluntary nature of the scheme. The scheme also means that more children are in 'legal deserts' than previously.

The Government has consulted on the scheme's voluntary interim transfer protocol, but are yet to publish the final version. Some local authorities have estimated that, despite an increase last year, Home Office funding is only meeting around 50% of the true costs of supporting a child for already stretched local authorities. This has resulted in some local authorities pulling out of the scheme. However, the Government have just announced to regularly review this funding.

Child detention continues in worsening conditions

In 2016, 103 children were locked up in immigration detention compared to 128 in 2015, with 42 under the age of 11. Last year the Government closed the specialist family detention unit, Cedars, and has started detaining children in a new family unit at Tinsley House Immigration Removal Centre, a secure detention centre. It is particularly concerning that this is now run by security company G4S, who have been criticised by the Home Affairs Select Committee for providing: 'disgraceful standards of asylum accommodation', and that the children's charity Barnardo's will no longer provide welfare support.

Cedars was built as part of the Government's pledge in 2010 to end the detention of children for immigration purposes, therefore closing it is a retrograde step. Since Cedars closed in October 2016, five children were housed in Tinsley House. However the family unit was closed for refurbishment in the last quarter. Another 19 were held in other centres since Cedars closed. Although the numbers of children detained are decreasing, this still breaks the Government's promise. This year, members of the Human Rights Council reiterated the UN Committee's oft-repeated call to end immigration detention for children.

Numbers of age-disputed children continue to rise

In 2016, 928 unaccompanied children had their age disputed – almost one-third of all children seeking asylum. This is an 18% increase on top of the 148% last year, but may be attributed to the increase in overall numbers, as the proportion has stayed stable. This shows that children are still constantly disbelieved about how old they are and face harmful, protracted age disputes despite calls from the UN Committee, which states: 'Age assessments should only be conducted in cases of serious doubt.' Again, children from four countries (Afghanistan, Iraq, Iran and Eritrea) account for 73% of age-dispute cases.

The Home Office's Assessing Age policy allows for individuals claiming to be children to be treated as adults if their appearance/demeanour: 'strongly suggests they look significantly over 18', despite the inherent difficulties in judging age based on appearance. Evidence from our members and

recent case law suggests this means they are frequently denied education, local authority support as a child, and housed or detained with adults. This is despite statutory guidance on unaccompanied migrant children, which states: 'where the age of a person is uncertain and there are reasons to believe they are a child, that person is presumed to be a child'. Age assessment guidance by the Association of Directors of Children's Services (ADCS) also states that children should have access to local authority support as a looked after child whilst the age assessment process continues, as set out in recent case law.

Data from the Refugee Council reveals that the number of children who are being detained as adults on the basis of their appearance has reduced this year (attributable to recent case law), but shows children are still being wrongly detained on the basis of physical appearance.

Slow progress on Dublin III

A child's right to reunite with their family is enshrined in Article 10 of the United Nations Convention on the Rights of the Child (CRC). The Government has made some progress in reuniting unaccompanied children with family members already in the UK under Dublin III: 700 children from Europe were reunited in 2016 compared to very few in 2015.

However, the Council of Europe and British Red Cross have documented that the length of time taken to complete the Dublin process and the lack of information available to children (particularly after the clearance of the camp in Calais in October 2016) meant that vulnerable children were left at risk in informal refugee camps in northern France, or were taking risky journeys in the hands of smugglers, even when they had family connections in the

UK. In addition, there is no clear or consistent best interest determination process to aid in children transferring to the UK.

When the UK leaves the EU, the Dublin III regulation will become inoperable. This will prevent unaccompanied asylum-seeking children joining their parents or other relatives residing in the UK. The UK has no comparable provisions to allow a child to enter the UK and have their protection claim determined here, and provides only for the reunification of parents and children where the former are recognised as refugees. There are many cases where children remain separated from their family members.

Closure of scheme to relocate children from Europe

We were extremely disappointed that in February 2017, the Government decided to close the scheme to relocate vulnerable unaccompanied children from Europe to the UK under S67 of the Immigration Act (the 'Dubs amendment'), citing local authority capacity as a key reason for the closure. The scheme has so far only welcomed 200 children, with a cap of total places at 480, and introduces a cut-off date of March 2016 for children to have been present in the EU. Organisations have expressed dismay that this is just a fraction of the amount they expected – or that the Government originally pledged. Discussions are ongoing with France, Greece and Italy over eligibility criteria and time frames, but as a result, very few additional children have been relocated to the UK since.

Unaccompanied children still separated from their families

The UK, unlike almost every other country in the EU, still does not allow children with refugee status to sponsor their parents to join them. This is despite the fact they have been

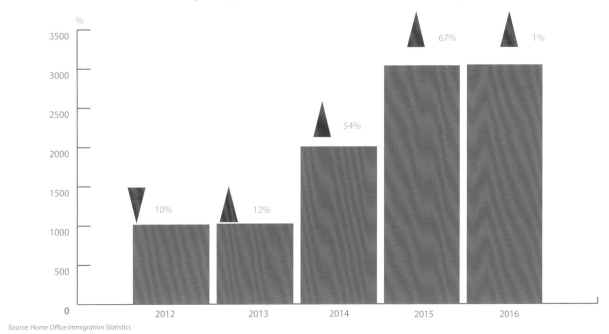

Asylum applications from unaccompanied children

Year	Value	%
2012	~1050	10% ▼
2013	~1050	12% ▲
2014	~2050	54% ▲
2015	~3050	67% ▲
2016	~3050	1% ▲

Source: Home Office Immigration Statistics

through an asylum determination process in the same way as an adult. Echoing a recommendation from the UN Committee, the members of the Human Rights Council urged the UK to: 'establish family reunification for child asylum seekers relocated to the UK or who have been recognised as refugees'.

Brexit a threat to EU children's residence rights

In 2016, 679,000 European national children under the age of 18 resided in the UK. A significant proportion of these children live here long term and around 258,000 (38%) were born in this country. Brexit poses significant risks for the rights of EU national children. The Government has set out plans where the right to stay is based on demonstrating five years of continuous and "lawful" residence. Many children will be denied residence rights, because they are reliant on their parents to demonstrate lawful residence or to complete the application for the new settled status, which children have no control over. There are no impact assessments on how this will affect vulnerable families, nor recognition of the need to consider the child's best interests, and the impact of European children being placed in care or being separated from their parents. Current application rates for non-EU citizens are complex and expensive with no free legal aid.

Table 1: Unaccompanied children's status and nationalities in 2016							
	Total	Refugee Status	Humanitarian Protection	Discretionary Leave	UASC Leave	Family or Private Life	Refusals
Afghanistan	406	83	1	6	269	0	47
Eritrea	328	143	31	0	120	0	34
Albania	228	2	0	0	173	0	53
Iran	215	54	0	4	108	0	49
Iraq	160	35	16	0	76	0	33
Syria	64	50	1	1	7	0	5
Vietnam	61	36	0	0	22	0	3

Source: Home Office Asylum Statistics

Poor routes to regularisation for undocumented children

There are approximately 120,000 undocumented children in the UK – 65,000 of whom were born here. They are living in precarious situations because they are unable to secure permanent status in the UK and their rights are being breached in many ways. Without documentation, a child cannot work, open a bank account, or access sources of support (such as housing), and are cut off from college and university, often leaving them vulnerable to poverty and exploitation. Less than 15% of the population of undocumented children in the UK have been able to regularise their status (or have left the UK), meaning thousands are still living in legal limbo.

These children face a number of barriers: complexity of law and policy, lack of awareness and understanding about their status by social and education services, lack of free, quality legal representation (see *Briefing 2*), very high application fees with very limited fee waivers, and long delays to regularise status. Fees to regularise their status are prohibitive at £1,000– £8,000 over a ten-year period, increasing every year with no parliamentary scrutiny and making a profit for the Home Office. The current system is not fair, accessible or in the best interests of children, and pushes them into undocumented status. Crucially it breaches children's rights to develop and fully participate as citizens in the country that they know as home.

Trafficking

NRM still not embedded in child protection systems

The year-long pilot of a revised National Referral Mechanism (NRM) model involving multidisciplinary panels was a positive step. The Government has published the evaluation of the NRM, but it still contains no plans to implement reform in line with the UN Committee's recommendation that the NRM be: 'embedded in existing child protection procedures'. However, the commitment to explore how best to make the NRM decision-making process 'child friendly' is encouraging. We also welcome the Government's pledge to publish statutory guidance on cictim identification and support in line with section 49 of the Modern Slavery Act 2015.

A new survey with frontline professionals found a worrying 40% of respondents said that the NRM never or rarely ensures an appropriate safeguarding response for children. Only 6% of respondents felt that there was good awareness of the NRM amongst frontline professionals who work with children. And only 4% felt decisions about identification should not be multi-agency – as is the case in the Government's recently announced changes to the system whereby Home Office officials in a new department will make identification decisions about all victims, including children.

High numbers of trafficked children going missing from care

New research based on FOI data from local authorities has revealed that more than a quarter of all trafficked children and over 500 unaccompanied children went missing at least once from September 2014–2015, and that 207 had not been found. It revealed a worrying lack of consistency in the way local authorities identify and record the risk of trafficking and exploitation, with no national process for identifying and recording children who may have been trafficked and who have gone missing. However, we welcome measures set out in the new 'Safeguarding unaccompanied asylum seeking and refugee children' strategy to work with local authorities who have high numbers of missing unaccompanied children, to understand and identify risk factors and effective responses, and to pilot a standardised process for police when they first encounter an unaccompanied child.

Shortcomings in 'non-punishment' provisions for child victims of trafficking

New research has found extreme variations in awareness of the 'non-punishment' provisions and how they can ensure that children who may have been trafficked are not criminalised, falling short of the UN Committee's recommendations. Where there is a proactive approach to identifying children by police and prosecutors, the provisions are making a difference. However, the research found few safeguards against arrest or prosecution at early stages of the criminal justice process, and very low levels of awareness of the non-punishment protections for children among prosecutors, police, defence solicitors and frontline practitioners. There was also little monitoring of the use of the presumption against prosecution or the statutory defence provision (introduced by the Modern Slavery Act 2015) for children across the UK.

December 2017

⇨ The above information is reprinted with kind permission from Children's Rights Alliance for England. Please visit www.crae.org.uk for further information.

©2018 Children's Rights Alliance for England

Children should be more involved in healthcare decisions that affect them

An article from **The Conversation.**

THE CONVERSATION

By Imelda Coyne, Professor of Children's Nursing, Trinity College, Dublin

Few people would disagree that children have a right to participate in matters that affect them. But in hospitals this right seems to be waived. My research at hospitals in Ireland revealed that children find it difficult to have their views heard.

The children said that doctors and nurses were 'nice' and 'kind', but some tended to carry out medical procedures without seeking their opinions or telling them beforehand. Some parents helped children to be included in talks about their care, but other parents answered questions on their behalf, told them to stay quiet and withheld information from them. Some parents also told their child to stay quiet and not annoy the doctor or nurse. Being excluded from discussions made some children feel sad, frustrated and angry. As one 14-year-old girl put it: 'It made me feel like a piece of machinery; they weren't actually talking to me.'

Big and small decisions

Children tend to see decisions as being big or small. They generally accept that adults make the 'really big' decisions and they trust them to make the right call. Children tended to trust their parents as they have their welfare at heart, and they believe that healthcare professionals know what the best treatment is as they are the experts. Nevertheless, children said that they would like to be included in discussions about decisions that affect them. They also expressed a desire for adults to use simple words – not medical jargon.

According to children, the 'small decisions' are those that focus on the way the nursing care, procedures and tests are done to them. For many children, though, these are important decisions because having choices makes it easier to cope. Inclusion in decisions, makes children feel happier, respected, less anxious and more prepared. Most children, regardless of age, prefer to share decision making with their parents and healthcare professionals rather than have sole responsibility.

Respecting human rights

Children and teenagers need to be involved in decisions as it respects their rights as human beings and makes it easier for them to cope with receiving care in hospital. Being in hospital can make children scared and anxious, but they are less likely to be distressed if they are prepared for what is going to happen to them.

Drafted by the UN nearly 30 years ago, the Convention on the Rights of the Child states that children have the right to be heard in all matters affecting their lives. Although there has been significant efforts to respect and promote the rights of children, they still encounter barriers to having their views heard in decisions that affect them.

Healthcare professionals and parents don't always agree on the extent to which children should be involved in making decisions about their treatment. Doctors and nurses want to provide the best care and treatment but worry about children's mental ability and emotional maturity to participate in decisions. As a result,

some healthcare professionals restrict the involvement of children in decisions that could influence the outcome of treatment for the worse.

Likewise, parents want the best for their child. They want to make the hospital stay easier for the child and for their child to get better and return home. Parenting practices have changed greatly over the past 30 years, and we now know that parents tend to listen more and include their children in everyday decisions in the home. In the hospital, many parents think it is important to involve children in decisions to promote self-esteem and well-being. But some parents feel they should protect their child from potentially distressing information or difficult decisions, so they restrict their child's involvement. They think that the child has enough to cope with, so they filter the information to avoid causing further distress.

However, we should not be overly critical of parents and healthcare professionals who exclude children from healthcare decisions as these decisions are not always straightforward and can vary a lot depending on the situation. Children often want to participate in discussions about their care but would rather not bear full responsibility for decision making.

When we talk about healthcare decisions most people think of major decisions that make the headlines, such as end-of-life decisions or legal capacity to consent. For children, though, it is about taking part, voicing preferences, being listened to and being heard in the decisions that affect their lives in hospital. These may be simple, but they can make a huge difference to children.

19 April 2017

⇨ The above information is reprinted with kind permission from *The Conversation.* Please visit www.theconversation.com for further information.

A summary of the UN convention on the Rights of the Child

Article 1 (definition of the child)

Everyone under the age of 18 has all the rights in the Convention.

Article 2 (non-discrimination)

The Convention applies to every child without discrimination, whatever their ethnicity, gender, religion, language, abilities or any other status, whatever they think or say, whatever their family background.

Article 3 (best interests of the child)

The best interests of the child must be a top priority in all decisions and actions that affect children.

Article 4 (implementation of the Convention)

Governments must do all they can to make sure every child can enjoy their rights by creating systems and passing laws that promote and protect children's rights.

Article 5 (parental guidance and a child's evolving capacities)

Governments must respect the rights and responsibilities of parents and carers to provide guidance and direction to their child as they grow up, so that they fully enjoy their rights. This must be done in a way that recognises the child's increasing capacity to make their own choices.

Article 6 (life, survival and development)

Every child has the right to life. Governments must do all they can to ensure that children survive and develop to their full potential.

Article 7 (birth registration, name, nationality, care)

Every child has the right to be registered at birth, to have a name and nationality, and, as far as possible, to know and be cared for by their parents.

Article 8 (protection and preservation of identity)

Every child has the right to an identity. Governments must respect and protect that right, and prevent the child's name, nationality or family relationships from being changed unlawfully.

Article 9 (separation from parents)

Children must not be separated from their parents against their will unless it is in their best interests (for example, if a parent is hurting or neglecting a child). Children whose parents have separated have the right to stay in contact with both parents, unless this could cause them harm.

Article 10 (family reunification)

Governments must respond quickly and sympathetically if a child or their parents apply to live together in the same country. If a child's parents live apart in different countries, the child has the right to visit and keep in contact with both of them.

Article 11 (abduction and non-return of children)

Governments must do everything they can to stop children being taken out of their own country illegally by their parents or other relatives, or being prevented from returning home.

Article 12 (respect for the views of the child)

Every child has the right to express their views, feelings and wishes in all matters affecting them, and to have their views considered and taken seriously. This right applies at all times, for example during immigration proceedings, housing decisions or the child's day-to-day home life.

Article 13 (freedom of expression)

Every child must be free to express their thoughts and opinions and to access all kinds of information, as long as it is within the law.

Article 14 (freedom of thought, belief and religion)

Every child has the right to think and believe what they choose and also to practise their religion, as long as they are not stopping other people from enjoying their rights. Governments must respect the rights and responsibilities of parents to guide their child as they grow up.

Article 15 (freedom of association)

Every child has the right to meet with other children and to join groups and organisations, as long as this does not stop other people from enjoying their rights.

Article 16 (right to privacy)

Every child has the right to privacy. The law should protect the child's private, family and home life, including protecting children from unlawful attacks that harm their reputation.

Article 17 (access to information from the media)

Every child has the right to reliable information from a variety of sources, and governments should encourage the media to provide information that children can understand. Governments must help protect children from materials that could harm them.

Article 18 (parental responsibilities and state assistance)

Both parents share responsibility for bringing up their child and should always consider what is best for the child.

Governments must support parents by creating support services for children and giving parents the help they need to raise their children.

Article 19 (protection from violence, abuse and neglect)

Governments must do all they can to ensure that children are protected from all forms of violence, abuse, neglect and bad treatment by their parents or anyone else who looks after them.

Article 20 (children unable to live with their family)

If a child cannot be looked after by their immediate family, the Government must give them special protection and assistance. This includes making sure the child is provided with alternative care that is continuous and respects the child's culture, language and religion.

Article 21 (adoption)

Governments must oversee the process of adoption to make sure it is safe, lawful and that it prioritises children's best interests. Children should only be adopted outside of their country if they cannot be placed with a family in their own country.

Article 22 (refugee children)

If a child is seeking refuge or has refugee status, governments must provide them with appropriate protection and assistance to help them enjoy all the rights in the Convention. Governments must help refugee children who are separated from their parents to be reunited with them.

Article 23 (children with a disability)

A child with a disability has the right to live a full and decent life with dignity and, as far as possible, independence and to play an active part in the community. Governments must do all they can to support disabled children and their families.

Article 24 (health and health services)

Every child has the right to the best possible health. Governments must provide good quality health care, clean water, nutritious food, and a clean environment and education on health and well-being so that children can stay healthy. Richer countries must help poorer countries achieve this.

Article 25 (review of treatment in care)

If a child has been placed away from home for the purpose of care or protection (for example, with a foster family or in hospital), they have the right to a regular review of their treatment, the way they are cared for and their wider circumstances.

Article 26 (social security)

Every child has the right to benefit from social security. Governments must provide social security, including financial support and other benefits, to families in need of assistance.

Article 27 (adequate standard of living)

Every child has the right to a standard of living that is good enough to meet their physical and social needs

and support their development. Governments must help families who cannot afford to provide this.

Article 28 (right to education)

Every child has the right to an education. Primary education must be free and different forms of secondary education must be available to every child. Discipline in schools must respect children's dignity and their rights. Richer countries must help poorer countries achieve this.

Article 29 (goals of education)

Education must develop every child's personality, talents and abilities to the full. It must encourage the child's respect for human rights, as well as respect for their parents, their own and other cultures, and the environment.

Article 30 (children from minority or indigenous groups)

Every child has the right to learn and use the language, customs and religion of their family, whether or not these are shared by the majority of the people in the country where they live.

Article 31 (leisure, play and culture)

Every child has the right to relax, play and take part in a wide range of cultural and artistic activities.

Article 32 (child labour)

Governments must protect children from economic exploitation and work that is dangerous or might harm their health, development or education. Governments must set a minimum age for children to work and ensure that work conditions are safe and appropriate.

Article 33 (drug abuse)

Governments must protect children from the illegal use of drugs and from being involved in the production or distribution of drugs.

Article 34 (sexual exploitation)

Governments must protect children from all forms of sexual abuse and exploitation.

Article 35 (abduction, sale and trafficking)

Governments must protect children from being abducted, sold or moved illegally to a different place in or outside their country for the purpose of exploitation.

Article 36 (other forms of exploitation)

Governments must protect children from all other forms of exploitation, for example the exploitation of children for political activities, by the media or for medical research.

Article 37 (inhumane treatment and detention)

Children must not be tortured, sentenced to the death penalty or suffer other cruel or degrading treatment or punishment. Children should be arrested, detained or imprisoned only as a last resort and for the shortest time possible. They must be treated with respect and care, and be able to keep in contact with their family. Children must not be put in prison with adults.

Article 38 (war and armed conflicts)

Governments must not allow children under the age of 15 to take part in war or join the armed forces. Governments must do everything they can to protect and care for children affected by war and armed conflicts.

Article 39 (recovery from trauma and reintegration)

Children who have experienced neglect, abuse, exploitation, torture or who are victims of war must receive special support to help them recover their health, dignity, self-respect and social life.

Article 40 (juvenile justice)

A child accused or guilty of breaking the law must be treated with dignity and respect. They have the right to legal assistance and a fair trial that takes account of their age.

Governments must set a minimum age for children to be tried in a criminal court and manage a justice system that enables children who have been in conflict with the law to reintegrate into society.

Article 41 (respect for higher national standards)

If a country has laws and standards that go further than the present Convention, then the country must keep these laws.

Article 42 (knowledge of rights)

Governments must actively work to make sure children and adults know about the Convention.

⇨ The Convention has 54 articles in total. Articles 43–54 are about how adults and governments must work together to make sure all children can enjoy all their rights, including:

Article 45

UNICEF can provide expert advice and assistance on children's rights.

Optional Protocols

There are three agreements, called Optional Protocols, that strengthen the Convention and add further unique rights for children. They are optional because governments that ratify the Convention can decide whether or not to sign up to these Optional Protocols. They are: the Optional Protocol on the sale of children, child prostitution and child pornography, the Optional Protocol on the involvement of children in armed conflict and the Optional Protocol on a complaints mechanism for children (called Communications Procedure).

⇨ The above information is reprinted with kind permission from UNICEF. Please visit www.unicef.org.uk for further information.

© 2018 UNICEF

Parents who share pictures of their children on social media putting their human rights at risk, UN warns

By Olivia Rudgard, Social Affairs Correspondent

Parents who share pictures of their children on social media are putting their human rights at risk, the United Nations has warned.

The UN's special rapporteur Joseph Cannataci said that 'strong guidelines' were needed to preserve the rights of children whose parents upload video and images of them.

During a mission to the UK to assess the privacy situation he also found that kindergarten-age children were being surveilled using CCTV at school and in their bedrooms.

At a press conference on Friday he suggested there could be a rising number of cases involving children who argue their rights have been infringed because their parents had posted videos and images of them on the Internet.

'How do you deal with parents who insist on taking a video of their kids every single day and posting it on YouTube every single day?

'We've already seen the very first cases of kids suing their parents because of the stuff they have posted on Facebook about them,' he said.

He said some nurseries were using their use of CCTV as a 'selling point' for 'anxious parents to check what's going on'.

'This has been fuelled further by all the reports we've seen of abuse of patients in care homes, and people being caught on CCTV, and sometimes the same allegations have been made about children's facilities,' he added.

Mr Cannataci said that children 'require increased protection' from companies who collect and share their data, but his investigation had not yet established whether new legislation was required.

He also criticised Home Office plans to prosecute people who repeatedly view extremist material online, arguing that prosecuting people for 'looking' is close to creating a 'thought crime'.

29 June 2018

⇨ The above information is reprinted with kind permission from *The Telegraph*. Please visit www.telegraph.co.uk for further information.

UK plummets from 11th to 156th in global children's rights rankings

Britain accused of employing 'inadequate' provision for children's rights protection.

By May Bulman

The UK has been accused of employing 'inadequate' provision for children's rights protection after it fell dramatically in global rankings for child rights within a year, from 11th to 156th.

Serious concerns have been raised about structural discrimination in the UK, including Muslim children facing increased discrimination following recent anti-terrorism measures, and a rise in discrimination against gypsy and refugee children in recent years.

The UK now ranks among the bottom ten global performers in the arena of improving rights of the child, after it achieved the lowest-possible score across all six available indicators in the domain of Child Rights Environment (CRE), according to the *KidsRights Index 2017*.

The report, which collects data from UNICEF and the United Nations Committee on the Rights of the Child (CRC) to identify global trends in the arena of children's rights protection, rates the extent to which a country has implemented the general principles of the CRC and to which there is a basic infrastructure for making and implementing children's rights policies. Portugal is this year's global frontrunner.

The report's methodology is such that extremely poor performances in one domain cannot be compensated by higher scores in other areas, as all children's rights are deemed to be equally important.

In light of the findings, Lord Philip Hunt, shadow deputy leader of the House of Lords and shadow health spokesperson, accused the Government of 'inactivity' and 'inadequate service provision', urging it to do more to protect the rights of the child.

'This report exposes the inactivity of the current UK Government and inadequate service provision in this most important area of policy making: rights of the child,' Lord Hunt said.

'The UK is the sixth largest economy globally and therefore has the resources at its disposal to ensure that our children are adequately protected and cared for across multiple disciplines. Our children are our future and the barometer of our approach to social justice and the state of our society.'

Marc Dullaert, founder and chairman of the KidsRights Foundation, meanwhile urged the UK to treat non-discrimination as a policy priority, and to speed up the process of aligning its child protection laws with the Convention on the Rights of the Child at both the national and devolved levels, as well as in all crown dependencies.

'Discrimination against vulnerable groups of children and youths is severely hampering opportunities for future generations to reach their full potential,' Mr Dullaert said.

'Following the general election, the new government should demonstrate to the world that it will not allow the retreat from the EU to adversely affect the rights and opportunities of its children.'

The Kids Rights Index, which assesses countries' commitments to children's rights relative to available resources, found that economically prosperous countries are not necessarily outperforming the rest. Poorer countries such as Thailand and Tunisia featured in the top ten, while more developed countries came far lower, with the UK and New Zealand among the bottom-ten global performers.

It concluded that industrialised nations were falling short of allocating sufficient budgets towards creating a stable environment for children's rights, by neglecting their leadership responsibilities and failing to invest in the rights of children to the best of their abilities.

On average, countries scored higher in the domain of Enabling Legislation, which measures the legal framework provided to protect and promote children's rights.

While many states have adopted new children's rights policies in recent years, the Kids Rights Index reveals that implementation is often lagging, and most new policies fail to fully comply with the principles and provisions of the CRC.

15 May 2017

⇨ The above information is reprinted with kind permission from *The Independent*. Please visit www.independent.co.uk for further information.

Ministers urged to close loophole which saw 50,000 children go 'missing' from education last year

By Camilla Turner, Education Editor

Ministers have been urged to close a loophole which saw 50,000 children go 'missing' from schools last year, leaving them exposed to radicalisation, trafficking and exploitation.

There is no national database that records Children Missing Education (CME) – those who are not registered as pupils at a school and are not receiving suitable education elsewhere – despite this group being at 'significant risk' of becoming 'victims of harm', according to official guidance.

It is up to local authorities to record data on CME, but the information they hold is patchy and many are unable to say whether these children are known to social services, according to research by the National Children's Bureau (NCB).

'The danger is that these are children who are potentially off the radar,' said Zoe Renton, head of policy and public affairs at the NCB, whose team carried out the research.

'These are children who aren't engaged with education, they may not be engaged with social services. The contacts that could be there to protect them to secure their welfare won't be there. We are missing out on opportunities to help vulnerable children.'

Last year there were 49,187 children reported as missing from education, according to data obtained from local authorities by the NCB, under freedom of information requests.

Statutory guidance for local authorities states that children reported as missing education are at 'significant risk' of 'underachieving, being victims of harm, exploitation or radicalisation'.

Anna Feuchtwang, chief executive of the NCB said it is 'alarming' that so

many children are missing education, adding that the Government must step up its efforts to protect this group.

The NCB's report, which will be launched this week, urges ministers to collect and analyse national-level data on CME, and review statutory guidance on how local authorities collect and record information on this.

Anne Longfield, the Children's Commissioner for England, said the research exposes how thousands of children are being failed because the system allows them to 'fall through the gap'.

She told *The Sunday Telegraph* that it is 'particularly shocking' that the Government does not even know for sure how many.

Ms Longfield said there must be better data collection and a 'real determination' from local and national government to identify children not in education 'both to stop this happening in the future and to provide better protection for those who the system is currently letting down'.

Cllr Richard Watts, Chair of the Local Government Association's Children and Young People Board, said that councils have 'long held concerns' that children missing school may not be receiving a suitable education.

Local councils are required to make 'reasonable enquiries' to establish the whereabouts of a pupil who has not attended school for 20 consecutive days before removing the child from the register.

Cllr Watts said he welcomed a recent change to statutory guidance means schools must now inform local authorities if a pupil is taken off the register, but added that laws still need to be stronger.

'While this helps councils both identify children at risk and unregistered schools, we believe a duty on parents to register home educated children with local councils would further help councils meet their safeguarding duties,' he said.

When children are taken off a school's register, local councils should also be informed about the destination school and family's home address, he said.

A Department for Education spokesperson said: 'Councils already have a duty to intervene if there are safeguarding concerns or if they believe children are not receiving a safe and suitable education.

'We are due to revise the guidance for local authorities and parents on the roles and responsibilities of educating children at home.'

27 January 2018

⇨ The above information is reprinted with kind permission from *The Telegraph*. Please visit www.telegraph.co.uk for further information.

Judge says US must seek consent to medicate immigrant kids

Afederal judge ruled Monday that the U.S. Government must seek consent before administering psychotropic drugs to immigrant children held at a Texas facility.

U.S. District Judge Dolly M. Gee in Los Angeles issued a ruling that the Federal Government violated portions of a longstanding settlement governing the treatment of immigrant children caught crossing the border.

Ms Gee said the Government must obtain consent or a court order to give children psychotropic medications at a Texas facility under state law unless it's an emergency.

She also said officials must tell children in writing why they are in a secure facility and that gang affiliation alone doesn't justify such a placement.

'The kids weren't getting notice of why they were sent away,' said Holly Cooper, co-director of the Immigration Law Clinic at University of California, Davis,

and one of the lawyers representing detained immigrant children. 'We view this as a victory.'

The decision comes as the Trump administration has toughened policies toward immigrant children and families caught crossing the U.S.-Mexico border. Immigrant rights advocates have fought back against many of the administration's moves, including separating immigrant parents and children.

The Department of Justice declined to comment on Ms Gee's ruling.

Immigrant children caught crossing the border alone are placed in government-contracted facilities until they can be released to screened sponsors in the United States or returned to their countries. Most children are placed in non-secure shelters, but in some cases, more secure placements are used.

In her decision, Ms Gee said she agreed with some but not all requests made

by the children's advocates. While some issues relate to the use of psychotropic drugs and the treatment of children at the Shiloh Treatment Center in Texas, the settlement governing detention conditions is overseen by the federal court in Los Angeles.

Immigrant and children's advocates also have filed a separate lawsuit in an effort to obtain greater oversight over how and when immigrant children are placed and kept in secure facilities, Ms Cooper said.

31 July 2018

⇨ The above information is reprinted with kind permission from *The Telegraph*. Please visit www.telegraph.co.uk for further information.

© *Telegraph Media Group Limited 2018*

World Day Against Child Labour

As part of a joint global campaign throughout 2018, the World Day for Safety and Health at Work (SafeDay) and the World Day Against Child Labour (WDACL) will focus on the need to end child labour and to improve the safety and health of young workers.

All children have the right to be free from all forms of child labour and all workers have the right to safe and healthy workplaces. Globally, 541 million young workers (between the ages of 15 and 24) account for 15 per cent of the world's labour force. They sustain up to 40 per cent more non-fatal occupational injuries than do adult workers (workers older than 24) and workplace hazards can even pose a threat to their lives. An estimated 152 million children (aged 5–17) around the world are in child labour, of whom 73 million perform work which is hazardous because of its nature or the circumstances in which it is carried out. Many factors contribute to hazardous child labour and the high rate of work-related injury and ill health among children and young workers. What is certain is that much more can and must be done. The campaign aims to accelerate action to achieve Sustainable Development Goal (SDG) Target 8.8: 'protect labour rights and promote safe and secure working environments for all workers' by 2030; and SDG Target 8.7: 'take immediate and effective measures to… secure the prohibition and elimination of the worst forms of child labour and, by 2025, end child labour in all its forms'. Reaching these goals requires renewed commitment and integrated approaches to eliminating child labour and promoting a culture of prevention on occupational safety and health, particularly for young workers.

The campaign calls for co-ordinated action to:

⇨ Promote the universal ratification and application of key International Labour Organization (ILO) Conventions on occupational safety and health (OSH) and on child labour, in particular:

- Occupational Safety and Health Convention, 1981 (No. 155);

- Safety and Health in Agriculture Convention, 2001 (No. 184);

- Promotional Framework for Occupational Safety and Health Convention, 2006 (No. 187);

- Minimum Age Convention, 1973 (No. 138); and

- Worst Forms of Child Labour Convention, 1999 (No. 182).

⇨ Promote integrated strategies at all levels to end hazardous child labour and address the specific safety and health risks faced by young workers.

⇨ Ensure quality education for all children and integrate occupational safety and health into general education and vocational training programmes.

⇨ Strengthen the evidence base for improved policies and actions to eliminate hazardous child labour and improve the safety and health of young workers.

⇨ Ensure that young workers gain access to trade union membership and are able to exercise their right to freedom of association, collective bargaining, and safety and health at work.

⇨ Address the specific vulnerabilities of the youngest children and prevent their entry into child labour.

⇨ Build stronger tripartite action to improve occupational safety and health for young workers and eliminate hazardous child labour, drawing on the experience of employers' and workers' organisations.

Young workers and children face very significant risks at work

Young workers and children are especially vulnerable to workplace hazards. They are much less able than adults to assess risk and, because they are still growing, are more vulnerable to hazards. Of course, children should

approach to eradicating all child labour. More attention must be paid to the youngest children (five-to 11-year-olds) for whom progress has stalled and among whom hazardous work has increased since 2012. We will never end child labour while children continue to enter child labour in the first place.

⇨ National lists of hazardous work that is prohibited for children should include work which is hazardous by its nature or because of the circumstances in which it is carried out.

⇨ All children below the age of 18 and engaged in work designated as hazardous should be removed from that work. If the work is inherently hazardous or if there is general or ambient risk, the child should be removed from the workplace altogether. Otherwise, protecting a child above the legal minimum age for work may require re-assignment to other, non-hazardous work in the workplace. In either case, the child has the right to complete basic education and, where appropriate, to receive quality vocational education and training.

⇨ With tripartite agreement, national authorities may authorise types of work listed as hazardous for those 16 years or older on condition that their health, safety and morals are fully protected and that they have received adequate instruction or vocational training in the relevant branch of activity. This enables young workers, for example, to learn occupations that require the use of potentially dangerous tools. However, personal protective equipment – besides being the least preferred means of workplace protection – is inappropriate for children: a small helmet cannot make

not perform types of work for which they have not reached the legal minimum age for the type of work concerned. However, children above the general minimum age for work and under 18, and young workers up to the age of 24, continue to develop physically and psycho-socially. Their stage of development, limited work experience, and lack of job skills together increase the risk that they face of suffering harm on the job. Moreover, young workers and children are the least able of all workers to speak up in the face of danger at work. Consequently, workplace safety and health must be promoted for workers of all ages, and most urgently for those who suffer disproportionally because of their youth.

Eliminating hazardous child labour and improving the safety and health

of young workers will make it possible for the next generation to start their working lives as productive, fairly-remunerated workers capable of contributing to social justice and economic growth. It will also improve the safety and health of all workers and help secure the livelihoods of parents and family members, thereby helping prevent child labour.

Ending child labour and promoting safe and healthy work for young people requires an integrated strategy:

For children under the age of 18:

⇨ Children in child labour must be withdrawn from all forms of work for which they have not reached the minimum age, and ensured access to quality education. Hazardous child labour must be prioritised as part of an integrated

underground mining acceptable for a child nor can a small hazmat suit permit a child to safely spray pesticides.

For young workers (18 to 24 years old):

⇨ In principle, similar provisions should apply to young workers aged 18–24, who, like all workers, have the right to refuse to perform work that presents immediate danger to their safety or health. Their engagement in permitted hazardous occupations should be subject to strict risk management, supervision and training.

⇨ All young workers should, in any case, be protected by an integrated strategy that promotes a culture of prevention for their benefit and seeks to identify and eliminate occupational safety and health hazards or, using age-appropriate interventions, control the risks of identified hazards:

- Young workers should receive basic OSH training before being assigned to perform job tasks

- Young workers should be fully trained in their job tasks and provided appropriate on-the-job supervision

- The right of young workers to refuse to perform work that presents an imminent danger to their safety or health must be protected.

June 2018

⇨ The above information is reprinted with kind permission from the International Labour Organization. Please visit www.ilo.org for further information.

Child labourers exposed to toxic chemicals dying before 50, WHO says

Bangladesh tannery workers exposed to formaldehyde, sulphuric acid and more while making products for westerners

By Sarah Boseley, Health Editor

Children as young as eight, working in the tanneries of Bangladesh producing leather that is in demand across Europe and the USA, are exposed to toxic chemical cocktails that are likely to shorten their lives, according to a new report.

Approximately 90% of those who live and work in the overcrowded urban slums of Hazaribagh and Kamrangirchar, where hazardous chemicals are discharged into the air, streets and river, die before they reach 50, according to the World Health Organization.

Their plight spurred the volunteer doctors of Médecins Sans Frontières (MSF) to set up clinics in the area to diagnose and treat those who are the victims of their workplace. It is, says a paper published in *BMJ Case Reports*, 'the first time they have intervened in an area for reasons other than natural disasters or war'.

MSF's intervention was triggered by 'the widespread industrial negligence and apathy of owners of tanneries and other hazardous material factories' towards the more than 600,000 largely migrant population who have no access to government-funded healthcare.

MSF set up and ran four main clinics for 5,000 workers in 2015, located in the centre of communities involved in four different manufacturing processes at factories for tanning, plastics recycling, garment-making and metals.

The hazards of the 250 or so tanneries in Hazaribagh – which are 30 to 35 years old and discharge 6,000 cubic metres of toxic effluent and ten tonnes of solid waste every day – are best known. In 2012, Human Rights Watch produced a report called *Toxic*

Tanneries which revealed the flouting of Bangladesh's own laws as well as international law in the employment of children under 18 in work that is harmful or hazardous.

The factories douse animal skins in cauldrons of chemicals as part of the processing of 'Bengali black' leather, which is exported to European leather goods manufacturers in Italy, Spain and elsewhere.

'Apart from heavy metals like chromium, cadmium, lead and mercury, a conglomerate of chemicals are discharged by the tanneries into the environment,' says the paper. 'Workers aged eight and older are soaked to the skin, breathing the fumes for most of the day and eat and live in these surroundings throughout the year. Personal protective equipment [is] not provided.'

Child workers clad in no more than loin cloths and wellington boots are exposed to chemicals including formaldehyde, hydrogen sulphide and sulphuric acid, write Venkiteswaran Muralidhar, associate professor at the Sri Balaji Medical college in Chennai, and colleagues

Child labour 'rampant' in Bangladesh factories, study reveals

The other factories – for plastics recycling, garments and metals – are in Kamrangirchar, an urban slum which is not officially part of Dhaka city. 'In these, there are complex risk hazards from cotton dust, heavy metals and chemicals like mercury, phthalates, acids and dioxins and ergonomic hazards,' says the paper.

Chronic skin and lung diseases are common, say the authors. Within six months of the setting up of the clinics, 3,200 of the 5,000 eligible workers had come forward for at least one consultation. Among them, 468 (14.6%) were diagnosed with suspected work-related diseases, and 30 (0.9%) had work-related injuries.

The figures do not reflect the overall harm to the population, however, said Muralidhar. Those who are severely injured by chemicals or accidents would not go to one of the clinics. 'They will probably be taken by rickshaw to a hospital in Dhaka,' he told *The Guardian*. And the clinics were only open four days a week, during the daytime, and workers needed the owner's permission to go for a consultation.

He feels strongly that a hospital should be set up in the slum to help its people. 'They are the most horrible conditions you can imagine,' he told *The Guardian*. 'I work in this area. I have never seen anything as bad as this.'

21 May 2017

⇨ The above information is reprinted with kind permission from *The Guardian*. Please visit www.theguardian.com for further information.

Child labour

In the world's poorest countries, around one in four children are engaged in child labour.

Children around the world are routinely engaged in paid and unpaid forms of work that are not harmful to them. However, they are classified as child labourers when they are either too young to work or are involved in hazardous activities that may compromise their physical, mental, social or educational development. The prevalence of child labour is highest in sub-Saharan Africa. In the least-developed countries, around one in four children (ages five to 17) are engaged in labour that is considered detrimental to their health and development.

The issue of child labour is guided by three main international conventions: the International Labour Organization (ILO) Convention No. 138 concerning

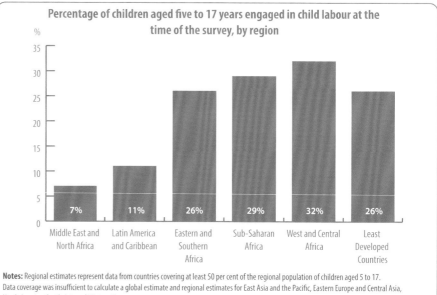

Percentage of children aged five to 17 years engaged in child labour at the time of the survey, by region

Middle East and North Africa: 7%
Latin America and Caribbean: 11%
Eastern and Southern Africa: 26%
Sub-Saharan Africa: 29%
West and Central Africa: 32%
Least Developed Countries: 26%

Notes: Regional estimates represent data from countries covering at least 50 per cent of the regional population of children aged 5 to 17. Data coverage was insufficient to calculate a global estimate and regional estimates for East Asia and the Pacific, Eastern Europe and Central Asia, North America, South Asia and Western Europe.

Source: UNICEF global databases, 2017, based on Demographic and Health Surveys (DHS), Multiple Indicator Cluster Surveys (MICS) and other nationally representative surveys, 2010–2016.

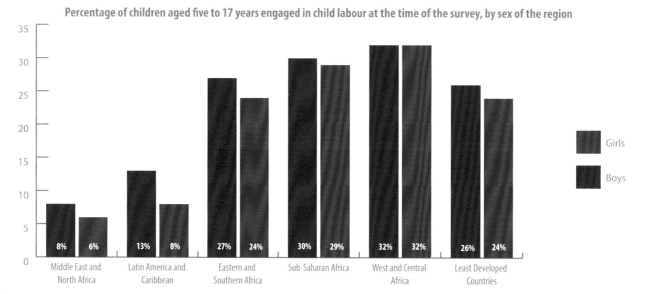

Percentage of children aged five to 17 years engaged in child labour at the time of the survey, by sex of the region

Middle East and North Africa: Girls 8%, Boys 6%
Latin America and Caribbean: Girls 13%, Boys 8%
Eastern and Southern Africa: Girls 27%, Boys 24%
Sub-Saharan Africa: Girls 30%, Boys 29%
West and Central Africa: Girls 32%, Boys 32%
Least Developed Countries: Girls 26%, Boys 24%

Notes: Regional estimates represent data from countries covering at least 50 per cent of the regional population of children aged 5 to 17. Data coverage was insufficient to calculate a global estimate and regional estimates for East Asia and the Pacific, Eastern Europe and Central Asia, North America, South Asia and Western Europe.

Source: UNICEF global databases, 2017, based on DHS, MICS and other nationally representative surveys, 2010-2016.

minimum age for admission to employment and Recommendation No. 146 (1973); ILO Convention No. 182 concerning the prohibition and immediate action for the elimination of the worst forms of child labour and Recommendation

No. 190 (1999); and the United Nations Convention on the Rights of the Child. These conventions frame the concept of child labour and form the basis for child labour legislation enacted by countries that are signatories.

Prevalence of child labour

Sub-Saharan Africa has the largest proportion of child labourers (29 per cent of children aged five to 17 years). In the Middle East and North Africa, fewer than one in ten (seven per cent) of children in this age group are performing potentially harmful work compared to 11 per cent of children in Latin America and the Caribbean.

In the world's poorest countries, around one in four children are engaged in work that is potentially harmful to their health

Gender disparities

In almost all regions, boys and girls are equally likely to be involved in child labour. A notable exception is Latin America and the Caribbean, where boys are slightly more likely than girls to be engaged in child labour. Gender disparities are observed, however, in the types of activities carried out, with girls far more likely to be involved in domestic work.

In most regions, girls are as likely as boys to be engaged in child labour

December 2017

⇨ The above information is reprinted with kind permission from UNICEF. Please visit www.data.unicef.org for further information.

© 2018 UNICEF

Modern slavery and child labour: it's all about choice

By Cindy Berman

We know that modern slavery and child labour are crimes and can never be tolerated. But they are also complex problems and tackling them boils down to the question of the choices people make.

The children, women and men who end up in situations of modern slavery are denied their fundamental right to choose their employer or to leave their place of work.

They are often coerced, threatened and deceived, and have little choice about the type of work they do, their pay, the hours they work, or the ability to keep themselves safe.

Companies face important choices about how they respond to forced labour and child labour. With many different factors driving and contributing to the problem, even the most responsible companies face dilemmas in knowing what choices to make in how they should respond.

For example, a zero-tolerance policy might lead a company to cut and run from a supplier where modern slavery is found. But they should also know that this does not necessarily help matters.

If the problem is endemic to a country, an industry or a sector, what would be achieved if they pulled out? They would most likely find similar situations in other factories or farms.

And where would it leave workers?

Workers can be far more vulnerable to abuse and exploitation if they and their family are desperate for the income. As such, they are often simply forced to seek employment elsewhere in circumstances that can be even worse.

Workers' vulnerability to abuse and exploitation

Seemingly well-meaning but knee-jerk reactions to 'rescue' a child or adult from a situation of forced labour can often end up victimising the worker even more:

⇨ Alerting an employer may result in greater abuse for the worker and threats to their family.

⇨ The employer or agent might abscond and scupper any possibility of a prosecution.

⇨ *And*, if the worker is a migrant, they could be locked up or deported with no rights or entitlements to compensation.

Workers who are the victims of modern slavery are not often asked what they want or given a choice about what lies ahead for them.

Governments too have important choices in how much they are willing and able to protect workers' rights.

Unfortunately, some are more concerned with protecting the private sector from any form of regulation in the mistaken belief that this will stimulate growth.

Modern slavery thrives where governments choose not to care too much. Not to care about protecting the basic rights of their citizens who make up the labour force of their countries. Not to care about who is exporting workers to earn an income for their families back home.

Some governments are constrained by their own capacity or resources. Yet governments from wealthier countries have a choice about how they invest their international resources, and how they expend their political capital by raising human rights issues in their trade and foreign policy dialogue.

Dealing with forced and child labour

Whilst forced labour and child labour are indeed complex, there are ways to deal with it.

Companies can make better and more informed choices about the decisions and actions they take, and they should know where to go for help when the problem lies beyond their own immediate control.

It's much easier (and far better of course) to prevent it from happening in the first place. Engaging with trade unions to enable workers to organise and negotiate their own terms and conditions of work is a key example of this, and would be more sustainable in the long term.

ETI has produced two new Guidance Reports – one on Modern Slavery (focusing on forced labour) and one on Child Labour to give practical advice and guidance.

These Guides will help companies better understand the problem and how to make informed choices about how to tackle it. They provide practical guidance on how to identify, manage and mitigate the problem, on how to understand their individual and collective responsibilities and how to remediate workers whose rights have been violated.

Modern slavery is not a new agenda for ETI.

The ETI Base Code of labour standards was established almost 20 years ago, and this guidance seeks to provide advice on two key clauses:

⇨ Clause 1: Employment is freely chosen

⇨ Clause 4: Child Labour shall not be used.

Forced labour and child labour sit at the extreme end of a continuum of exploitation and abuse of workers.

But these labour rights abuses are related to the denial of other workers' rights, such as the right to freedom of association, living wages, reasonable working hours, job security and freedom from discrimination.

The Base Code is based on ILO Conventions, and these are heavily referenced in the Guides.

But there is a long distance between international instruments that state what is acceptable in international and domestic law and the actual implementation of these conventions – particularly in the context of complex supply chains in an increasingly globalised economy.

Going further than the Base Code

The Guides go further than explaining what the Base Code clauses mean.

They also set out a practical approach for companies using the ETI Human Rights Due Diligence Framework. This is a framework based on the UN Guiding Principles on Business and Human Rights that recognises governments' responsibilities to protect workers from exploitation and abuse, companies' responsibilities to respect workers' rights and for workers to get remedy when their rights are violated.

Whatever the circumstance, the protection of workers themselves

must be the first consideration for companies and governments – whether they are children or adults. They need to be consulted and supported in whatever action is taken to remove them from harm, and to ensure that their basic ability to earn a decent living is protected.

The guides are aimed at companies. They contain useful advice, examples, explanations and references for more information.

But each situation of modern slavery is different and responses will need careful analysis, often requiring expertise and partnerships. As such the guides do not provide standard templates or blueprints but will guide companies in their actions and choices.

We invited experts to be lead authors.

The Modern Slavery Guide has been developed in partnership with Anti-Slavery International, with Klara Skrivankova as the lead author. Mike Dottridge, is a child labour, slavery and human rights expert was the lead author of the Child Labour guidance.

Both have decades of experience advising governments, multilateral bodies, companies, and have worked in the field with victims of child labour and forced labour.

5 July 2017

⇨ The above information is reprinted with kind permission from Ethical Trading Initiative. Please visit www.ethicaltrade.org for further information.

The glitter victims: Indian children suffer for the mining of cosmetic material mica

'We dug with our bare hands. We found my younger daughter who had clawed and dragged herself out of the soil despite her broken leg. 'But Laxmi was dead by the time we found her, she was not breathing. There was no life in her.' Sitting outside their mud home in Duba village, in eastern India, Parwatiya Devi recounts the last moments she saw her 12-year-old daughter Laxmi Kurmari, who had died in a collapsed mine eight months ago. Her ten-year-old daughter who sits next to her, can still barely walk.

The girls weren't playing in an abandoned mineshaft, they were working – searching for the once lowly mineral known as mica. The sparkly material is used to add glitter to everything from car paint to eyeshadow.

Fatal conditions

India is one of the largest producers of the silver-coloured material and many children like Laxmi have died each year working in horrendous conditions to mine it.

India's mica industry once boasted more than 700 mines and over 20,000 workers. It was hit by legislation in the 1980s as the Government moved to limit deforestation and the discovery of substitutes for natural mica forced most mines to close.

But renewed interest driven by China's booming economy and a global craze for 'natural' cosmetics saw illegal operators reopen abandoned mines, creating a lucrative black market.

In Jharkhand and Bihar states, some of the poorest regions of India, children as young as five are part of an opaque supply chain – beginning in Giridih's decrepit mines and ending in London's fragrant beauty stores.

Indian law forbids children below the age of 18 working in mines and other hazardous industries, but many families living in extreme poverty rely on children to boost household incomes which average around 200 rupees (£2.50) a day.

Campaigners estimate this illegal trade accounts for some 25 per cent of the global production of mica and involves up to 50,000 child workers in India.

Holistic solutions

An initiative to end child labour in India's mica industry by 2022 was established in January and backed by multi-billion-pound companies. But it has failed to have any tangible effect on the ground, campaigners say.

Jos de Voogd, from Terre des Hommes, a children's rights charity in The Netherlands, said: 'It is really important to look at the problem in a holistic way if you want to solve this problem.

'Simply banning children from working is not a solution, you have to ensure that their parents are paid good wages so they can make a living and don't have to send children to the mines. This is the Government's responsibility, although something that companies can obviously help with (and have responsibility for).'

The Responsible Mica Initiative (RMI) – whose 39 members include cosmetics firms Estee Lauder and L'Oreal, and German drugs and chemical group Merck KGaA – has raised little funds. Village activities to curb child labour have not yet started either.

'The RMI is an initiative with a lot of promise, yet it has in the last year failed to live up to that promise,' said Sushant Verma from Nobel Laureate Kailash Satyarthi Children's Foundation (KSCF), a charity working to end child labour in mica mines for over a decade that initially supported the RMI.

'Could the companies have done more? The answer is yes. They had a year and yet there is little to show on the ground. Children are dying in these mines, but there is no sense of urgency to really tackle the problem.'

Slow progress

The Paris-based RMI, however, said its first year was a "preparation year" dedicated to setting up the organisation, enlisting members and raising funds. Projects to improve the lives of rural communities are expected to begin next year.

'When I compare many other initiatives, it's incredible that already around 40 members have decided to join and take action altogether and have a five-year programme with real impact,' said RMI's Executive Director Fanny Frémont.

'I don't think it could have been done any quicker.' But Laxmi's family can take no solace from this and now their grief has turned to despair on realising promises by global companies to end child labour in the mines in eastern India have so far led to nothing.

'I don't know about any company coming and helping here. I don't even know what this mica is used for,' said Parwatiya.

'But even with the death of my child and three others in this village, people are still sending their children to collect mica. That's all we have. There is nothing else.'

Hidden toll

The discovery that seven children had died in the region in two months alone prompted pledges by multinationals sourcing mica from India to clean up their supply chains, and state authorities vowed to accelerate plans to legalise and regulate the sector.

But campaigners fear the death toll is likely much higher than what is initially officially stated and the bodies of many victims are not recovered from the rubble, or are quickly and silently cremated in the forests by mine operators.

A Thomson Reuters Foundation's investigation in 2016 found child workers not only suffer injuries and respiratory infections but they risked being killed and their deaths hushed-up.

In some cases, the victims' families are threatened by mine operators or buyers not to report the deaths, or they are given 'blood money' to keep silent so the illicit industry continues.

RMI founding member, cosmetics firm L'Oreal – which states over 99 per cent of its mica comes from 'legal gated mines' free of child workers – said companies will begin divulging supply chain details when the technology is piloted next year.

'Our ambition with our partners and the RMI is to achieve a compliant and fair mica sector in India over the next five years,' a L'Oreal spokesperson said.

22 December 2017

⇨ The above information is reprinted with kind permission from iNews. Please visit www.inews.co.uk for further information.

Slaves on our streets: child labour 'staring us in the face' in British shops, says Penny Mordaunt

International Development Secretary warns consumers about the grim realities of the global supply chain.

By Arj Singh

The products of modern slavery "stare at us in the face" as we shop on Britain's high streets, the International Development Secretary has said.

Penny Mordaunt said: 'It is possible that the clothes we wear, the electronics we use and the food we eat could be the product of child and forced labour' in businesses' supply chains around the world.

She set out how Britain would spend £40 million of funding pledged by Prime Minister Theresa May in September to help more than 500,000 vulnerable men, women and children who have either survived modern slavery or are at risk of becoming victims.

Part of the package will go towards targeting problem sectors such as the garment industry, fisheries and construction.

Ahead of the International Day for the Abolition of Slavery on Saturday, Ms Mordaunt said: 'In the world we live in, it is as easy to traffic people as drugs or guns and not enough is being done to tackle it. This is a global disgrace.

'While we continue to tackle the slavery still present in the UK, the only way for us to eradicate the practice once and for all is to tackle the problem both in the UK and at its source, stamping it out of our economies.

'The additional support we are setting out today will help vulnerable people who face the horrific and daily reality of modern day slavery.

'It will help people who want to earn a decent living and support their families, but end up being forced, coerced and deceived into working against their will in factories, in the sex trade and in the hidden world of domestic slavery.

'Without action, the results of the modern slavery industry will continue to stare us in the face as we walk down British high streets.

'It is possible that the clothes we wear, the electronics we use and the food we eat could be the product of child and forced labour, and this undermines legitimate businesses and economic development which are lifting thousands of people out of poverty.

'It is absolutely imperative that we work both at home and abroad to make certain that we are breaking the business model of people perpetrating an evil abolished by Britain 200 years ago.'

The Ethical Trading Initiative, which is partly funded by the Department for International Development, said 77 per cent of the companies it surveyed last year thought there was a likelihood of modern slavery occurring in their supply chains.

Asda, Ikea, John Lewis, Marks & Spencer, British Airways, Nestlé and Tesco were among the companies willing to be named as participants in the research, although the report did not state whether they thought modern slavery could occur in their supply chains.

The package of UK aid includes £13 million to prevent trafficking and forced labour among women migrant workers in South Asia, which has the

highest prevalence of forced labour in the world, and will focus on victims of forced domestic work and garment manufacturing.

There is also a £20 million contribution to the Global Fund to End Modern Slavery, which will be used to target problem sectors such as the garment industry, fisheries and construction, combating slavery by working with law enforcement, prevention and victim services, and businesses.

A further £7m will be allocated for victim support, awareness raising and law enforcement in Nigeria, which is one of the main source countries for trafficking to the UK, often in the sex trade.

1 December 2017

⇨ The above information is reprinted with kind permission from The Press Association. Please visit www.independent.co.uk for further information.

How gangs are exploiting children to do their dirty work

THE CONVERSATION

An article from **The Conversation.**

By Grace Robinson, Graduate Teaching Assistant, Edge Hill University

Children as young as 12 have been reported to be doing drug runs in London. Targeting the most vulnerable young people in society – usually looked-after children or those already known to social services – organised crime gangs are using grooming tactics to coerce, manipulate and force young children into criminality to pay off unwanted debts.

Through my ongoing research with Youth Offending Teams, who work with young people in trouble with the law, I've found that young people are initially given cannabis, alcohol and cigarettes as a reward for helping with

gangs' dirty work. This can encourage addiction and once addicted, gang members tally up the cost of the drugs, allowing young people to quickly accumulate large debts. Vulnerable young people are becoming trapped in a situation where committing crime is one of very few ways that they can pay off their debt to the gang.

The majority of them fail to realise that they are being manipulated and exploited. My continuing research with staff in youth offending services has found that victims of this new kind of grooming believe that their criminal activity is one of 'choice', and that by complying, gangs will respect them

and give them a sense of belonging. Sadly, I've heard that this rarely materialises and through the use of violence and intimidation, gangs exert control and a level of ownership over the young person from which it is difficult to escape.

County lines

Though gangs are typically highly territorial, laying claim over an area or postcode, they have expanded by moving into areas outside of major cities. This has resulted in the new phenomenon of 'county lines'. This typically involves gangs from urban areas transporting class A drugs such as heroin and crack cocaine to

underdeveloped drug markets in small counties and coastal towns. Exploited young people are used as the main transporters of these substances. One man from Peckham, South London, was convicted in January for running a gang supplying drugs in Plymouth.

Criminal exploitation is not, however, restricted to drugs, and there is evidence that some young people are transporters of cash as well as knives and firearms.

A report published in 2016 by the National Crime Agency was the first to acknowledge criminal exploitation in gangs, particularly through the use of county lines. The report detailed how organised crime gangs use mobile phone lines to forge a deal between drug users and drug mules. The phones are kept away from the drug supply and a relay system is put in place where the young person will deliver drugs, pick up cash and return to the urban location to begin the cycle again.

Drug users, addicts and vulnerable girls living in small counties are also exploited to assist with dealing and are commonly forced to use their homes as a base for storing drugs and weapons.

While London gangs are the dominant exporters to county lines, other gangs are reportedly travelling from Liverpool, Manchester and Birmingham. One particular gang from Merseyside has reportedly been the supplier of drugs across Lancashire, West Yorkshire, Devon and Cornwall.

Plans to 'crack down'

In late January, the Government announced plans to crack down on the county lines run by gangs. An amendment was tabled to the Digital Economy Bill, currently making its way through parliament, that would force phone providers to disconnect mobiles and SIM cards believed to be connected with drug offences.

Officials have estimated that a single phone line has the ability to generate up to £3,000 per day, and so the number of SIM cards thought to be used for this purpose, an estimated £2 million a week.

But with growing demand and increased levels of criminal organisation, it is unlikely that the Government's efforts will disrupt the drugs supply and infiltration of gangs into smaller towns. The removal of one gang will only create a void to be filled by another, which could encourage a vacuum of violence in the process as members fight to get to the top.

The political focus on tackling this kind of child criminal exploitation is clearly welcome. Society once treated those children groomed for sexual exploitation as offenders of 'child prostitution'. These attitudes have changed over the past decade due to greater political attention on tackling child sexual exploitation.

We now immediately recognise the victim of child sexual exploitation as a child – and this ought to be the case for those criminally exploited by gangs. Instead, law enforcement agencies are criminalising victims of this exploitation, drawing them into a system of intense scrutiny and powerlessness. Society is now running the risk of criminalising the most vulnerable. There has already been evidence of this through the use of Joint Enterprise, a 'lazy law' which has allowed the courts to criminalise gang members for slight association with a gang.

The line between victim and offender has become too blurred to separate. So next time you hear of a young person being branded as a feral gang member, dig a little deeper and look for evidence that challenges your prejudices and assumptions.

1 February 2017

⇨ The above information is reprinted with kind permission from *The Conversation*. Please visit www.theconversation.com for further information.

How high street clothes were made by children in Myanmar for 13p an hour

Children of 14 were working a six-day week.

By Gethin Chamberlain

Children as young as 14 have been employed to make clothes for some of the most popular names on the UK high street, according to a new report.

New Look, Sports Direct's Lonsdale brand and H&M have all used factories found to have employed children, after several major brands switched their production to low-cost factories in Myanmar. Workers told investigators that they were paid as little as 13p an hour producing clothes for UK retailers – half the full legal minimum wage.

Labour rights campaigners say that the use of children in factories supplying household names is the result of a 'race to the bottom', as brands chase ever lower labour costs.

The Netherlands-based Centre for Research on Multinational Corporations (known by its Dutch initials as Somo) interviewed 400 workers in 12 factories supplying international brands and worked with *The Observer* to finalise the report.

'We thought that brands were getting the message on child labour but this investigation shows the risks involved in constantly trying to cut labour costs,' said researcher Pauline Overeem. 'The widespread use of children in Myanmar to manufacture clothes for western brands is alarming and depressing and we urge all companies to take responsibility and to ensure that children are getting the education they need and deserve.'

Brands have had some success eliminating child labour from their main supplier factories in recent years, but as wages have risen in countries such as China, companies are increasingly moving production to cheaper markets, including Myanmar, where children can legally be employed for up to four hours a day from the age of 14.

The legal minimum wage in Myanmar is 3,600 kyat (£2.12) for an eight-hour day – equivalent to 26p an hour. Workers in all the factories investigated worked six-day weeks. Labour NGOs argued when the minimum wage was set that a minimum of 6,000 kyat a day was required for a basic standard of living.

All the factories investigated employed workers below the age of 18. Several workers at factories supplying Lonsdale and New Look stated in detailed interviews that they had started work at the age of 14.

A German brand that sourced from the same factory as New Look reported that it had found 'misconducts' at the factory, including evidence of child employment. Researchers said the factory subsequently dismissed all workers below the age of 18. But one of the workers, asked her age by the researchers, replied: 'Do you want to know my real age or my age at the factory?' A worker at another factory told researchers: 'When buyers come into the factory the child workers are being told not to come to work that day.'

There were also reports of several workers below the age of 15 at a factory supplying H&M and Muji. H&M confirmed that it had found two 14-year-olds but that an inspection in November found no one under 14.

Researchers found wages below the full legal minimum at factories supplying Sports Direct, Henri Lloyd, New Look, H&M, Muji, Pierre Cardin and Karrimor (owned by Sports Direct).

The lowest wages of just 13p an hour were found in factories supplying H&M, Karrimor, Muji and Pierre Cardin. The day rate for those workers was £1.06. Myanmar's labour laws permit factories to pay newer workers at reduced rates.

Workers say they struggle to live on such low wages. Thiri and Yadana, who both worked at a factory supplying Lonsdale, said they could only afford to live in a makeshift hut in a squatter area without electricity or running water.

Thiri said: 'The upside of living here is that we don't need to spend money on rent which makes it easier to get by.'

According to Myanmar's factories act, workers should not be expected to do more than 60 hours a week, including overtime, but workers reported longer hours in factories supplying New Look, Sports Direct, Henri Lloyd, Karrimor and H&M. Forced overtime was reported by workers in factories supplying H&M, Muji, Sports Direct and Henri Lloyd, while there were reports of unpaid overtime at factories supplying New Look, Pierre Cardin and H&M.

Factory owners in Myanmar say they are under intense pressure from brands to cut costs. Daw Khine Khine Nwe, secretary of the Myanmar Garment Manufacturers Association, urged UK shoppers to think about how budget clothes are produced. 'We are asking the buyer to increase the rate and we'll share it with the worker. But they're not willing.'

In an interview with *The Observer* in Yangon last year, she said: 'The consumer also needs to understand – the consumer asks for better quality but when it comes to the price they always look for the cheapest one. Which do you want?'

The low labour costs in Myanmar have encouraged international brands to switch production from more expensive countries and between 2010 and 2014 exports tripled to £787 million. There are now more than 400 factories in the country, employing 350,000 people, 90% of them women.

In its report, Somo urges the companies to pay workers a living wage: 'Clothing companies are constantly on the lookout for production locations that can make clothes quickly and at low costs,' it says. 'Over the past few years, Myanmar has rapidly become a popular sourcing destination for the garment industry due to a huge pool of cheap labour and favourable import and export tariffs.

However, working conditions in this industry are far from acceptable. Labour rights violations are rife. Asian suppliers are setting up shop in Myanmar in an unseemly 'race to the bottom', pushed by foreign buyers that are eager to secure the cheapest possible prices.'

New Look said: 'We recognise the issues highlighted in this report. We are working with our suppliers and local partners in Myanmar to address the findings and to support the development of an ethical garment industry in the area.'

H&M said the report raised 'industry-wide challenges'. 'It is of utmost importance to us that all our products are made under good working conditions and with consideration to environment, health and safety. We want people to be treated with respect and that our suppliers offer all their workers good, fair and safe working conditions.'

The company stressed that child labour was totally unacceptable, but pointed out that the legal age for working in Myanmar was 14.

Sports Direct dismissed the interviews with the workers as 'anecdotal and uncorroborated', with a spokesman adding: 'We would therefore strongly advise you not to publish.' But in a statement the company said: 'However, we do not condone these types of abuse and we have policies in place which reflect this view. Details of these policies are published on our company website in our statement about the Modern Slavery Act.'

A spokeswoman for Muji said: 'We are committed on a global scale to always ensure good working practices, both internally and in cooperation with our external partners.'

Pierre Cardin said it would investigate the matter further and take the appropriate measures.

Henri Lloyd did not respond to repeated requests for comment and did not respond when offered an opportunity by Somo to react to the report.

5 February 2017

⇨ The above information is reprinted with kind permission from *The Guardian*. Please visit www.theguardian.com for further information.

Child marriage

Child marriage is a violation of human rights, but is all too common

Marriage before the age of 18 is a fundamental violation of human rights. Many factors interact to place a girl at risk of marriage, including poverty, the perception that marriage will provide 'protection', family honour, social norms, customary or religious laws that condone the practice, an inadequate legislative framework and the state of a country's civil registration system. Child marriage often compromises a girl's development by resulting in early pregnancy and social isolation, interrupting her schooling, limiting her opportunities for career and vocational advancement and placing her at increased risk of domestic violence. Child marriage also affects boys, but to a lesser degree than girls.

Cohabitation – when a couple lives 'in union', as if married – raises the same human rights concerns as marriage. When a girl lives with a man and takes on the role of his caregiver, the assumption is often that she has become an adult, even if she has not yet reached the age of 18. Additional concerns due to the informality of the relationship – in terms of inheritance, citizenship and social recognition, for example – may make girls in informal unions vulnerable in different ways than girls who are married.

The issue of child marriage is addressed in a number of international conventions and agreements. The Convention on the Elimination of All Forms of Discrimination against Women, for example, covers the right to protection from child marriage in article 16, which states: 'The betrothal and the marriage of a child shall have

no legal effect, and all necessary action, including legislation, shall be taken to specify a minimum age for marriage….' The right to 'free and full' consent to marriage is recognized in the Universal Declaration of Human Rights, which says that consent cannot be 'free and full' when one of the parties involved is not sufficiently mature to make an informed decision about a life partner. Although marriage is not mentioned directly in the Convention on the Rights of the Child, child marriage is linked to other rights – such as the right to freedom of expression, the right to protection from all forms of abuse, and the right to be protected from harmful traditional practices – and is frequently addressed by the Committee on the Rights of the Child. Other international agreements related to child marriage are the Convention on Consent to Marriage, Minimum Age for Marriage and Registration of Marriages, the African Charter on the Rights and Welfare of the Child and the Protocol to the African Charter on Human and People's Rights on the Rights of Women in Africa.

Child marriage among girls

Across the globe, levels of child marriage are highest in sub-Saharan Africa, where around four in ten young women were married before age 18, followed by South Asia, where three in ten were married before age 18. Lower levels of child marriage are found in Latin America and the Caribbean (25 per cent), the Middle East and North

Africa (17 per cent), and Eastern Europe and Central Asia (11 per cent).

The prevalence of child marriage is decreasing globally, with the most progress in the past decade seen in South Asia, where a girl's risk of marrying in childhood has dropped by more than a third, from nearly 50 per cent to 30 per cent.

Still, the total number of girls married in childhood stands at 12 million per year, and progress must be significantly accelerated in order to end the practice by 2030 – the target set out in the Sustainable Development Goals. Without further acceleration, more than 150 million additional girls will marry before their 18th birthday by 2030.

Married adolescents

Globally, about one in six adolescent girls (aged 15 to 19) are currently married or in union. West and Central Africa has the highest proportion of married adolescents (27 per cent), followed by Eastern and Southern Africa (20 per cent) and the Middle East and North Africa (13 per cent).

Around one in four adolescent girls in West and Central Africa are currently married or in union, compared to 1 in 17 in East Asia and the Pacific.

Child marriage among boys

Child marriage affects girls in far greater numbers than boys, with the prevalence among boys about one

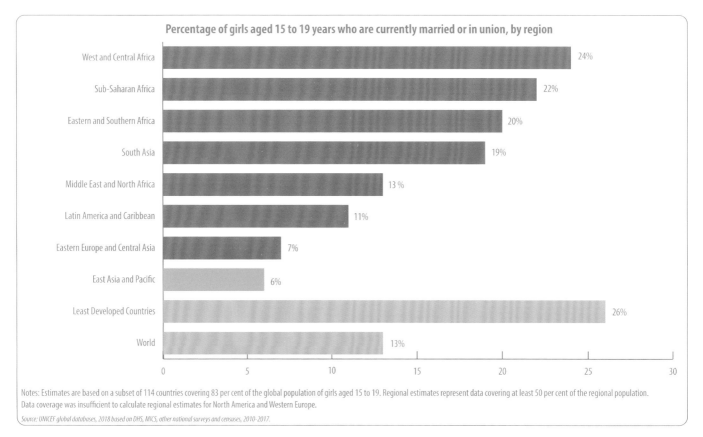

Percentage of girls aged 15 to 19 years who are currently married or in union, by region

Region	Percentage
West and Central Africa	24%
Sub-Saharan Africa	22%
Eastern and Southern Africa	20%
South Asia	19%
Middle East and North Africa	13%
Latin America and Caribbean	11%
Eastern Europe and Central Asia	7%
East Asia and Pacific	6%
Least Developed Countries	26%
World	13%

Notes: Estimates are based on a subset of 114 countries covering 83 per cent of the global population of girls aged 15 to 19. Regional estimates represent data covering at least 50 per cent of the regional population. Data coverage was insufficient to calculate regional estimates for North America and Western Europe.

Source: UNICEF global databases, 2018 based on DHS, MICS, other national surveys and censuses, 2010-2017.

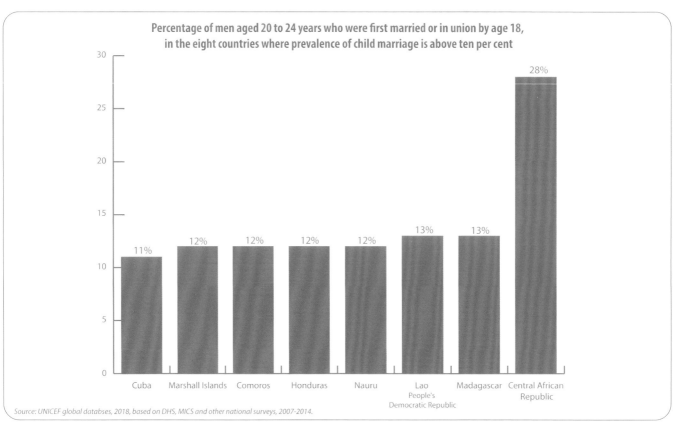

Percentage of men aged 20 to 24 years who were first married or in union by age 18, in the eight countries where prevalence of child marriage is above ten per cent

Country	Percentage
Cuba	11%
Marshall Islands	12%
Comoros	12%
Honduras	12%
Nauru	12%
Lao People's Democratic Republic	13%
Madagascar	13%
Central African Republic	28%

Source: UNICEF global databses, 2018, based on DHS, MICS and other national surveys, 2007-2014.

fifth the level among girls globally. Available data confirm that in every region boys are less likely than girls to marry before age 18, though there are countries in which boys marrying before age 18 is not uncommon. However, data on the number of boys affected by child marriage are limited, making it difficult to draw definitive conclusions on its status and progress.

In eight countries, more than ten per cent of boys are married before age 18.

March 2018

⇨ The above information is reprinted with kind permission from UNICEF. Please visit www.data.unicef.org for further information.

Eight child marriage myths that need to go

From the halls of the United Nations to communities around the world, much has been done to raise awareness of child marriage. But sometimes the myths about what drives child marriage persist. Here are eight common misconceptions about child marriage – and why they're wrong.

1 'Child marriage only happens in Africa and Asia'

A Google search for 'child marriage' will bring up photos of Indian brides or adolescent mothers from Africa. But child marriage is a global problem that cuts across countries, regions, cultures and religions. The countries with the highest numbers of child brides range from Niger to Indonesia to Brazil. The practice also happens in parts of North America and Europe.

2 'Child marriage is a cultural practice. We have to respect culture'

In many communities, child marriage has been a tradition for decades, if not centuries. So much so that it can be seen as a core part of the culture. But not all cultural practices are positive. Child marriage deprives girls of education and economic opportunities, and puts their health and safety at risk. The solution is not to condemn all traditions, but to work with communities to change traditions from within. As Girls Not Brides champion Graça Machel always says: 'Traditions are made by people, they can be changed by people.'

3 'Child marriage only happens to girls'

Child marriage is driven by gender inequality. But boys are married off too. According to UNICEF, 156 million men alive today were married before 18. Child marriage often pushes boys into the workforce and forces them to take on adult responsibilities before they are ready.

4 'Parents do not care for their daughters if they marry them off'

Child marriage is driven by factors that go beyond parents' individual decisions. Parents might feel they have no choice given the circumstances, or think they're doing the best for their daughters. Ignoring the root causes of child marriage, or attacking the value system of people who practise it, will only alienate girls and their parents. When parents see how much better off girls are in school and out of marriage we can create change.

5 'Child marriage always involves young girls and older men'

The media often focuses on stories of girls married at a very young age. While these stories happen, the vast majority of child marriages involve adolescent girls. Globally, the rates of marriage of under-15s have gradually declined. But the marriage rates of 16- to 17-year-old girls have stagnated or increased.

Behind this trend lie deeper problems: lack of educational and employment opportunities for girls past secondary school, as well as the social and family pressure to marry – especially if they already have a boyfriend. In Nepal, for instance, there has been an increase in 'love marriages' where adolescent boys and girls decide to marry.

6 'Child marriage is a family matter. It does not concern us.'

The consequences of child marriage do not just stay within the family. When 12 million girls are married before 18 every year, everyone is affected. Child marriage perpetuates cycles of poverty, inequality and oppression – from one generation to another. It is one of the most blatant manifestations of gender inequality worldwide. It should concern us all.

7 'Child marriage is a religious problem'

Child marriage is not linked to a single religion. It happens to girls of Hindu, Muslim or Catholic faith, as well as girls from other faiths. In fact, religious leaders play a crucial role in tackling child marriage. They can check that the bride and the groom are both above 18 before a religious wedding, promote progressive interpretation of religious texts, and help people understand that their religion does not condone child marriage.

8 'These girls must be completely helpless'

Girls can play a huge role in ending child marriage if they have access to education and know about their rights. Many girls who once faced child marriage, now advocate for an end to the practice. Girls speaking from experience are well placed to change the minds of their peers and community members.

The causes and drivers of child marriage are as varied as they are complex. And by constantly challenging the myths about child marriage and setting the record straight we are all a step closer to solving a problem that affects 15 million girls each year.

18 December 2017

⇨ The above information is reprinted with kind permission from *Girls Not Brides*. Please visit www.girlsnotbrides.org for further information.

Meet the men standing against child marriage

Kuuntunna is a farmer who has many dreams for his seven-year-old daughter. None of them involves seeing her become a child bride. Yet he fears this chilling prospect because he lives in a part of Ghana where many girls are abducted and forced into child marriage. Poverty and patriarchy drive the problem. But men can also be part of the solution. Meet four men who are standing with local women and ActionAid to tackle child marriage in northern Ghana.

The dad standing against child marriage

Sitting on the dusty porch of his daughter's school, Kuuntunna describes his hopes for her future.

'I wish that Porshia grows up to be a nurse or a teacher,' he said. 'I'm so happy that she goes to school, because I didn't go to school. So I wish that one day she grows up to be somebody more important than me.'

But Kuuntunna, who grows millet and guinea corn for a living, fears that Porshia's potential could be cut short by child marriage.

The family lives in the Upper West region of Ghana, where more than 50 girls have been abducted for marriage in a year.

'Marriage by abduction is something that is happening in the community,' said the 30-year-old. 'So I have that fear.'

The practice involves groups of men snatching girls who are on errands or travelling to school. The girls are taken to the men's villages and forced to marry one of them.

Many parents, who lack money and influence, feel powerless to confront the kidnappers because of the threat of violence.

ActionAid supports communities to bring back abducted girls

ActionAid works in the Upper West region, where more than 70 per cent of the population live on less than 68 pence a day .

Our work includes training groups of villagers – men and women – to bring back abducted girls. The groups, known as COMBAT (community based anti-violence teams) have been trained by the police to confront perpetrators.

This often involves approaching the abductors or their village chief and threatening legal action if the girls are not released. This type of pressure has proved effective.

More than 150 girls have been rescued by COMBAT in the past five years. COMBAT's presence is also vital in remote villages where the nearest police station is several hours' journey away.

Kuuntunna welcomes this support.

'If they take your daughter, you don't have the strength or money to get her back, so ActionAid's work matters,' he said.

The village chief standing up to child marriage

ActionAid's programme officer, Abiba, 31, has also been working with a network of influential male village chiefs to persuade them to fight child marriage.

Naa Mwinsaama Bondegbee the Second is a village chief in northern Ghana. He has attended several ActionAid workshops about child marriage.

When 14 girls from his village were abducted last year he took action, sending emissaries to secure the girls' release. The 69-year-old said this earned him enemies, but he believes that keeping girls in school is more important.

'If girls finish school and get good jobs, the name of our village will shine,' he said.

The granddad standing up to child marriage

When Dotto's granddaughter Fatima, 16, was abducted he sought help from school teachers, who have been trained by ActionAid to tackle child marriage.

They encouraged him to locate her. When Fatima's uncle and aunt brokered her release, men from the abductors' village brought her back to school.

OUR GIRLS NEED DREAMS

-NOT NIGHTMARES..

Dotto, 76, now wants Fatima to complete her education and contribute to her community. He grows maize, yam and groundnuts and earns around ten Ghanaian cedis (£1.80) a week.

'Educated people, people who have gone to school and are earning a salary, they are developing the world,' he said. 'I want Fatima to be one of them.'

The dad helping his daughter overcome the stigma surrounding child marriage

When Mustafa's 14-year-old daughter Anna, was abducted on the way home from school, he got help from ActionAid worker, Abiba. Abiba went to the abductors' village with the police and Mustafa and got Ama out.

'I was so happy when Ama was released because it means she can continue with her education and make her future better,' said Mustafa, 53.

Today Ama is a dedicated student who loves studying science. She is also a member of ActionAid-funded girls clubs. The clubs are led by female teachers who support the girls to talk about their problems and learn about their rights to resist all forms of violence.

But Ama, now aged 15, almost didn't return to school after her release. That's because some children teased her and called her a "new wife". Then, her dad gave her the pep talk she needed.

'My dad said those people laughing at me want me to drop out of school. He said they were just jealous of me,' Ama said. 'After that I wiped the tears from my face, got up and got my bathwater. When I finished bathing, I put on my uniform and went to school.'

Please support women and men in Ghana to continue fighting child marriage. A regular gift from you will help us to reach many more girls such as Ama and support the work of committed campaigners to help end child marriage.

21 July 2017

⇨ The above information is reprinted with kind permission from ActionAid. Please visit www.actionaid.org.uk for further information.

Child marriage laws are an important first step, but not sufficient

This is an extract from a published article.

By Quentin Wodon, Paula Tavares, Oliver Fiala, Alexis Nestour and Lisa Wise

Background

Child marriage is defined as a formal or informal union before the age of 18. The practice affects mostly girls. While child marriage is especially prevalent in low and lower-middle income countries, it is also observed in other countries. It endangers the life trajectories of girls in multiple ways. Child brides are at greater risk of experiencing a range of poor health outcomes, having children at younger ages when they are not yet ready to do so, dropping out of school, earning less over their lifetime, and living in poverty compared to their peers who marry at later ages. Child brides may also be more likely to experience intimate partner violence, have restricted physical mobility, and limited decision-making ability. Most fundamentally, child brides may be disempowered in ways that

deprive them of their basic rights to health, education and safety. These dynamics affect not only the girls themselves, but also their children and households, as well as communities and entire societies.

Child marriage is widely considered as a violation of human rights and a form of violence against girls. The elimination of child marriage by 2030 is a target under the Sustainable Development Goals (SDGs). Yet investments to end the practice are limited, and worldwide the incidence of child marriage has been declining too slowly over time to achieve the SDG target. Furthermore, in many countries, it remains legal to marry a girl before she turns 18, and even in countries where marriage before 18 is in principle illegal, too many girls continue to marry early.

The World Bank and Save the Children recently published a brief on the lack of legal protection against child marriage for girls and marriages that take place below the national minimum age of marriage. The analysis suggests that many countries still do not legally protect girls against child marriage, but also that legal reforms alone are not sufficient to end the practice as many girls marry illegally in countries where legal protections are in place. While protecting girls in the law against child marriage is an important first step, additional interventions are needed to prevent child marriage.

Lack of legal protection against child marriage

The threshold to define a child and thereby child marriage internationally is 18 years of age. This threshold is used in multiple conventions, treaties and international agreements, including the Convention on the Rights of the Child, the Convention on the Elimination of All Forms of Discrimination against Women, and the Universal Declaration of Human Rights. The threshold makes sense for several reasons. First, research suggests that girls younger than 18 are often too young for sexual, marital and reproductive transitions. Marrying before 18 can also have large negative impacts on a wide range of other outcomes for girls and their children. For example, 18 years corresponds in many countries to the age for completing secondary schooling. When girls marry early, it reduces the likelihood that they will be able to complete their secondary education. Furthermore, young girls are typically not legally capable of giving their free and full consent to their marriage.

In most countries, child marriage is prohibited by national law. Indeed, most countries have adopted 18 years as the legal age for marriage for girls, and in some countries the age is higher. But there are countries with a lower legal age for marriage. In addition, even when the legal age is 18 or higher, many countries allow girls to be married earlier if their parents or judicial bodies authorise it. The fact that in many countries there are no legal sanctions for those involved in child marriage may compound the issue. Where no sanctions exist, the law may be less effective in acting as a deterrent for the practice. Finally, in some countries, the minimum age for marriage is lower under customary or religious laws than national law, which also undermines legal protections. For these reasons, the law often provides limited protection against child marriage for girls.

Key results

Child marriage laws are important to provide girls with legal protection and signal commitment to achieving the Sustainable Development Goal target of ending child marriage by 2030. Most countries have adopted 18 as the legal age for marriage for girls, but many countries allow younger girls to marry with parental or judicial consent. Close to 100 million girls globally are not legally protected against child marriage when considering exceptions that allow marriage at a young age with parental or judicial consent. Between 2015 and 2017, nine countries improved their laws on the minimum age for marriage, typically by eliminating exceptions that allow child marriage with parental or judicial consent.

Yet while national laws against child marriage are important, they are not sufficient for ending the practice. Globally, even after accounting for exceptions to the legal age of marriage with parental or judicial consent, 7.5 million girls marry illegally each year (20,000 girls per day), making up 68 per cent of all child marriages. Beyond adopting laws setting the minimum age for marriage at 18 without exceptions, additional measures that address the underlying causes of child marriage and that expand access to quality education and other opportunities for girls need to be pursued more actively by governments with support from the international community.

⇨ The above information is reprinted with minor adaptation and with kind permission from The World Bank and Save the Children. Please visit www.worldbank.org for further information. The full brief on child marriage laws and their limitations is available at http://documents.worldbank.org/curated/en/334131513322505611/Ending-child-marriage-child-marriage-laws-and-their-limitations.

© The World Bank 2018

Economic costs of child marriage and low educational attainment for girls

This is a summary of recent research at The World Bank.

By Quentin Wodon

Background

There is a strong relationship between child marriage and educational attainment for girls. Child marriage is one of the leading reasons why girls drop out of school prematurely. Conversely, enabling all girls to complete their secondary education could virtually end, or at least dramatically reduce the prevalence of child marriage. Beyond this mutual relationship, child marriage and low educational attainment for girls both have large negative effects on a wide range of other development outcomes, as demonstrated in two recent studies by The World Bank. The first study, conducted by The World Bank in partnership with the International Center for Research on Women, focused on the economic costs of child marriage. The second study focused on the cost of not educating girls and is the focus of this brief summary.

Despite substantial progress over the last two decades, girls still have on average lower levels of educational attainment than boys in many countries, especially at the secondary and tertiary levels. As documented by the World Development Report 2018, when it comes to actual learning, while girls tend to outperform boys in reading, they score lower in maths and science tests in many countries. Together with occupational segregation and social norms that discourage women from taking full advantage of labour market opportunities, this leads to large gaps in earnings between men and women. In addition, low educational attainment for girls has potential negative impacts on a wide range of other development outcomes not only for the girls themselves, but also for their children, families, communities and societies.

As is the case for child marriage, low educational attainment affects girls' life trajectories in many ways. Girls dropping out of school early are more likely to marry or have children early, before they may be physically and emotionally ready to become wives and mothers. This may affect their own health. It may also affect that of their children. For example, children of mothers younger than 18 face higher risks of dying by age five and being malnourished. The children may also do poorly in school. Other risks for girls and women associated with a lack of education include intimate partner violence and a lack of decision-making ability in the household.

Through lower expected earnings in adulthood and higher fertility over their lifetime, a lack of education for girls leads to higher rates of poverty for households. This is due to both losses in incomes and higher basic needs from larger household sizes. Data on subjective perceptions also suggest that higher educational attainment is associated with perceptions of higher well-being among women.

Low educational attainment for girls may also weaken solidarity in communities and reduce women's participation in society. Lack of education is associated with a lower proclivity to altruistic behaviours, and it curtails women's voice and agency in the household, at work and in institutions. Fundamentally, a lack of education disempowers women and girls in ways that deprive them of their basic rights.

At the level of countries, a lack of education for girls can lead to substantial losses in national wealth. Human capital wealth is the largest component of the changing wealth of nations, ahead of natural capital (such as oil, minerals and land) and produced capital (such as factories or infrastructure). By reducing earnings, low educational attainment for girls leads to losses in human capital wealth and thereby in the assets base that enables countries to generate future income. The World Bank study on the cost of not educating girls suggests that barriers to completing 12 years of education for girls may cost countries between $15 trillion and $30 trillion dollars globally in lost lifetime productivity and earnings. The study also finds out that primary education is not enough. Across many indicators, benefits from primary education alone are limited.

Low educational attainment for girls is also associated with higher population growth given its potential impact on fertility rates. This may prevent some countries from ushering the transition that could generate the demographic dividend. Finally, low educational attainment for girls may lead to less inclusive policy-making and a lower emphasis on public investments in the social sectors. Overall, the message is clear: educating girls, and in so doing putting an end to child marriage, is not only the right thing to do. It also makes economic and strategic sense for countries to fulfil their development potential.

⇨ The above information is reprinted with minor adaptation and with kind permission from The World Bank and Save the Children. Please visit www.worldbank.org for further information. The full study on the cost of not educating girls is available at https://openknowledge.worldbank.org/handle/10986/29956.

© The World Bank 2018

A school is handing out metal spoons for girls to put in their underwear to prevent forced marriages

By Josh Barrie

A school is trying to combat forced marriages by giving students metal spoons to hide in their underwear.

Pupils at the Co-operative Academy in Leeds are being urged to do so as the steel cutlery would trigger metal detectors at airports.

It means children who fear they are being taken overseas to be married would be able to alert security staff privately.

Trigger airport metal detectors

Harinder Kaur, the school's social, culture and ethos leader, said 80 per cent of forced marriages involving young people based in the UK happen during the summer holidays, and said the spoons could "save lives".

She told the BBC: 'In the six-week holidays we know there is no contact between school and the family and families have that opportunity to go abroad, get their child married and come back,' she said.

'It's a way of making our children aware there is a safety net there.' In total, 1,000 spoons were given out to children at the Co-operative Academy. They were distributed by human rights charity Karma Nirvana (of which Ms Kaur is a patron), which campaigns against forced marriages, honour killings and abuse.

Criminal offence

MPs have this month debated how best to prevent forced marriages – and how schools can do more to keep vulnerable young people safe.

Forcing people into marriage became a criminal offence in the UK in June 2014. The law made it illegal to force two people into marrying against their will, and parents who attempt to see their children wed could face up to seven years in prison.

13 July 2018

⇨ The above information is reprinted with kind permission from iNews. Please visit www.inews.co.uk for further information.

NGOs need to step up and keep children safe – here's what they can do

An article from **The Conversation.**

By Rosa Freedman, Professor of Law, Conflict and Global Development, University of Reading

THE CONVERSATION

The wave of reports about abuses perpetrated by aid sector workers in Haiti and elsewhere, including allegations of the abuse of children, should sadly come as little surprise. International actors frequently fall into the gaps between national, regional and international law, and therefore need internal measures to ensure that they adhere to international standards. And of all the players in international interventions, NGOs perhaps need them the most.

Unlike militaries, intergovernmental organisations or even private sector actors, NGOs frequently have weak or non-existent governance structures. This extends to every part of their organisation, from recruitment all the way up to accountability mechanisms. And when locally employed staff abuse or exploit children in countries where the rule of law is weak or non-existent, there is little the organisations can do to to bring them to justice.

The solution is not to strictly curtail the aid sector's international activities; the world would be significantly worse off without the work many of these organisations do. Instead, the sector's practices and standards have to be brought into line so that fewer abuses occur. Above all, the people who work for NGOs need to understand what to do if they suspect or know that abuse has been perpetrated. And that can only be achieved with tough systemic reforms.

When it comes to a problem as highly charged as the abuse of vulnerable children, legal restrictions and safeguarding measures are frequently derided as plasters applied to bullet wounds, principally because they do not provide headlines to match the problems they're designed to solve. But without them, guaranteed long-term improvements are close to impossible.

Taking responsibility

Every organisation has a responsibility to ensure that children are safeguarded from harm. They must make sure that their staff, operations and programmes do no harm to children – that is, that they do not expose children to the risk of harm and abuse. That means they are obliged to report any safety concerns to the authorities in the communities where they're working.

But besides abiding by local laws and measures, organisations working internationally also need to observe regional and global ones. While definitions of 'child' and 'child abuse' differ across nations and cultures, this is not the point. NGOs need to adhere to international standards, and to be clear that the word 'children' encompasses anyone under 18, and that 'abuse' encompasses all acts that harm children – intentionally or otherwise.

It is incumbent on NGOs to comprehensively map the laws and safeguarding practices that apply in the countries where they operate. There need to be consultations with staff across the organisation in order to give clear guidance on these issues and how to respond when concerns arise. Yes, child safeguarding measures must be sensitive to the local culture – but the question of who is a child and what constitutes abuse is clearly set out in global and regional standards and frameworks, and it must be applied across the board.

This means that organisations must fully vet all staff during recruitment, and make safeguarding central to those processes. Staff must be made aware of the international laws and standards to which they are expected to adhere, and the repercussions for not doing so. There must be clear lines of reporting when staff suspect abuse or when allegations are made, including to local authorities where at all possible.

These might sound like small steps, but this systematic approach has worked in tens of thousands of organisations around the world. When NGO staff know how to recruit safely, all the way through to what is expected of them if they suspect abuse, there are fewer opportunities for abusers to perpetrate crimes. No organisation can ever guarantee it is free from abuse or abusers, but any organisation must do everything it can to minimise risks and maximise accountability.

The aid sector in general suffers from a culture of opacity and silence, as opposed to transparency and openness. As it tries to change that, there's plenty to learn from intergovernmental organisations and other international actors who've tried to clean up their act, and from organisations such as Keeping Children Safe, who provide safeguarding training. Rather than shouting on the sidelines about what they've seen happening elsewhere, everyone in the sector needs to play their part in implementing solutions that actually make a difference.

13 February 2018

⇨ The above information is reprinted with kind permission from *The Conversation*. Please visit www.theconversation.com for further information.

Missing education: the hidden children

By Anna Feuchtwang, Chief Executive of National Children's Bureau

The simple fact of the matter is too little is known about the thousands of children who are missing education. The only way to piece together a national picture of the children who drop off the school roll and don't receive a suitable education elsewhere (for example, through home schooling) is by conducting a freedom of information request – but the data returned by local authorities varies wildly.

The National Children's Bureau has published the best estimate possible about this hidden group of children, showing that 49,187 children were reported as missing education (CME) at some point in 2016/17.

And this isn't just about missing out on learning. These children are, to quote the Government guidance on the issue, at 'significant risk of underachieving, being victims of harm, exploitation or radicalisation, and becoming NEET', underlining that the impact on individual children can be acute.

I am struck by this fact when watching the animations we have produced to accompany publication of our research. These fill in some of the gaps about what we know about CME; to remind us all about the vulnerable children, often living chaotic lives, who lie behind the statistics.

Take July for example. July is a 14-year-old girl who found it difficult to make friends at primary school. Later diagnosed with autism, July started missing lessons in secondary school and then stopped attending school entirely. She started attending a special school but wasn't able to get the help she needed; she'd get into arguments with teachers and run away. The school kept suspending July because they said they couldn't keep her safe. With no other schools nearby that could help, July stopped attending school altogether and instead spends her time alone at home, while her mother is out at work.

Another example is Amil, a nine-year-old boy living with his mum, brothers and sisters. Short-term housing placements means that Amil moves house, and school, nearly every year. Sometimes he only spends a few weeks in a new home, so doesn't go to school at all. When he does attend a new school, it is hard for him to make new friends and he has no one to play with. When Amil finally gets a placement that lasts over a year, he starts to make friends and progress in his learning, but the threat of the next move is always hanging over him.

These stories are based on qualitative research that we conducted into the experiences of CME. This research found that a series of complex and often interrelated factors cause children to drop out of education.

It can be because of the individual child's feelings and experiences or mental health. It can be because of problems in the family, for example, domestic violence, family breakdown or caring responsibilities. Or it can be a problem with the school environment, such as the school not meeting the needs of a child with special educational needs or disabilities, unsuitable placements, unofficial exclusions or bullying. Finally, the problem might stem from wider issues such as moving to or from abroad, moving into a different local authority or to do with gender or cultural issues.

I was reminded reading through these stories that two common themes were often apparent in these children's lives. Often, the child was growing up in a low-income family, and there was also a likelihood that the child could have come to the attention of other services. This could have been because a risk of abuse or harm had been noted by social workers, or because other professionals had raised a concern, such as the police noting a child at risk of falling into crime.

This is borne out by the data from our latest Freedom of Information Request. As well as asking local authorities about the numbers of CME, we also asked whether these children were receiving free school meals and whether they were known to social services. While the availability of this data was patchy, we found that 22% of children recorded as CME were in receipt of free school meals when last on a school roll. This compares with only 13% of all children in the same local authorities. When it came to links with social care, data from 94 local authorities shows that 15% of children recorded as CME are known to social services. We don't have a figure for how many children across the country are 'known' to social services, but we do know that 5.5% of all children were referred to social services in 2016/17.

Again the data for both questions varies greatly between local authorities with no clear explanation why, but it seems that differences in data recording and collection may account for some of this variation.

This is frustrating in the extreme. These findings hint at the varied and profound challenges that children recorded as CME face, and underlines that they are clearly in need of urgent support. Yet national government does not even gather in one place the little data held at a local level.

The Government has a chance to act: the statutory guidance for local authorities is due for review in 2019 and must be updated to achieve a better standardisation of data, including information such as eligibility for free school meals and whether the children are known to social services, so that we get a better understanding of the overlapping vulnerabilities within this group.

Only when central government collects and publishes reliable local data on CME, will we start to understand this hidden group of children better, and have a better opportunity to support their route back into education and ensure their needs are met.

29 January 2018

Bleak film charts final days of Kayleigh Haywood in stark warning about online grooming

By Samuel Osborne

A bleak film which tells the story of how teenager Kayleigh Haywood was groomed online by a stranger and then brutally raped and murdered has been released by police.

The film, called *Kayleigh's Love Story*, charts the last fortnight of her life and warns parents and children of the dangers of online grooming.

Kayleigh, 15, was killed by Stephen Beadman in November 2015 after being bombarded with messages on Facebook and other social media sites for around two weeks by his 28-year-old neighbour Luke Harlow.

Over a fortnight, they exchanged 2,643 messages.

Harlow groomed Kayleigh, along with two other girls he had also been speaking to, but it was Kayleigh who finally agreed to his requests to spend the night at his house.

The five-minute short was made with the support of Kayleigh's parents and has already been shown at schools in Leicestershire and Rutland.

Leicestershire Police said 35 children found the courage to come forward and report possible cases of grooming to officers after seeing the film.

The award-winning film, which begins with a warning that it would have a 15 certificate if shown in a cinema, starts by showing how Kayleigh began receiving messages from Harlow.

As the pair exchange messages, the film cuts between scenes of Kayleigh at home with her family and Harlow smoking a cigarette in his flat.

It also shows examples of messages Harlow sent the teenage girl as he groomed her.

'Mum and dad wouldn't understand, they don't know that he's different,' the actress playing Kayleigh says.

The film shows Kayleigh meeting Harlow at his house on Friday 13 November, where she spent the next day.

In the early hours of Sunday 15 November, having been held against her will by Harlow and his next door neighbour Stephen Beadman, Kayleigh was raped and murdered by Beadman.

The video ends by warning: 'Stop and think. When you meet someone online, you don't always know who you are talking to.'

The film was shot in various locations across Leicestershire and Nottingham by Affixxius Films.

Miles Latham, managing partner of Affixxius Films, told *The Independent*: 'It is one of the most intricate projects we have ever taken on. The production of a film this graphically accurate, while the case was still going on, is unheard of.

'Very few police forces would have the courage to get the family's permission. There were obvious difficulties having to work with Kayleigh's mum and dad, which was incredibly difficult.

'They were obviously broken, hollow people. But to give them enormous credit, they were 100 per cent behind the project from the beginning. They endorsed the film wholeheartedly.'

He said the video agency wanted to capture the character of Kayleigh in the film. 'We wanted her to walk like Kayleigh, to move like Kayleigh, to interact with her family like Kayleigh did.'

Leicestershire Police gave them access to all of the digital messages exchanged between Kayleigh and Harlow, allowing them to build their script. 'It's like reading something out of a horror film,' Mr Latham said.

He said he hoped the film would 'reinforce a message which is as old as time: Don't talk to strangers'.

'The only way we can stop other incidences like Kayleigh's happening is if young adults have a moment of realisation and are able to realise that things could develop.'

Leicestershire's Deputy Chief Constable Roger Bannister said: 'What happened to Kayleigh was horrific but we are pleased that some good is coming from the awful tragedy and that this film is raising far greater awareness of the dangers of online grooming and the signs that it may be happening.'

Last July, Beadman, then 29, was sentenced to life imprisonment for the rape, false imprisonment and murder of the teenager, while Harlow was given a 12-year jail term for false imprisonment and grooming.

3 January 2017

Forced conversions of Hindu girls in Pakistan make a mockery of its constitution

***An article from* The Conversation.**

By Sadiq Bhanbhro

THE CONVERSATION

In a famous speech on 11 August 1947, Pakistan's founder and first governor general, Muhammad Ali Jinnah, stressed that the new country was being built on the idea of religious tolerance:

You are free; you are free to go to your temples, you are free to go to your mosques or to any other place of worship in this State of Pakistan.

But 70 years later, a trend of forced conversions in the country is making a mockery of the constitution of Pakistan, which offers equal rights to all religious minorities.

In early June, a 16-year-old Hindu girl called Ravita Meghwar was allegedly abducted by men in the southern Pakistani region of Sindh. Within hours, Ravita had apparently embraced Islam. She was given a new name – Gulnaz – and married off to a Muslim man.

The next day she told journalists that she had accepted Islam and married the man without any pressure. But Meghwar's parents reported the suspects, claimed she was a minor, and demanded the safe recovery of their daughter. Countering the claims, Meghwar's husband submitted an application to the Sindh High Court to seek protection from her family and relatives. The case was settled on 23 June when the Sindh High Court allowed Meghwar to go with her husband. The judge apparently ignored the 2013 Sindh Child Marriage Restraint Act which prohibits marriages under the age of 18.

In a similar case in early 2012, a young Hindu girl called Rinkle Kumari was victim of a forced conversion to Islam. The case went to court but ended with Kumari going to live with her husband.

A growing problem

Forced conversions to Islam have become a new form of violent extremism in Pakistan. A forced conversion is defined as being when any person uses pressure, force, duress or threat, to make another person adopt another religion. It affects almost all religious minority groups in Pakistan but Hindu teenage girls in the Sindh province are the main victims. There are no verified numbers but according to the NGO, South Asia Partnership Pakistan, at least 1,000 girls, mostly Hindus, are forcibly converted to Islam in Pakistan every year.

Conversion to Islam is a one-way process. Once a person becomes Muslim – forcibly or voluntarily – then going back will be an act of apostasy, which is punishable by death in Islam under penal law. There is no way for a person to go back due to an imminent danger of being killed.

I have done some initial analysis of English-language newspaper reports in Pakistan of forced conversions that occurred between January 2012 – just before the Kumari case – and June 2017. In total, I found reports of 286 separate incidents of women and girls being forcibly converted. The actual number could be much higher as many cases of forced conversion are reported in local Urdu or Sindhi newspapers. As one journalist working on the issue in Pakistan told me, many cases in which influential locals and religious leaders are involved go unreported because of pressure put on the media not to report the stories.

Even if families report the kidnappings to the police, the kidnappers usually file a counter report on behalf of the girl claiming she has come of her own will, has accepted Islam and is happily married. When they do take on the cases, the courts often find in favour of

the Muslim men. For example, in one case in 2016 involving a 16-year-old called Shabana, the Sindh High Court declared her marriage valid and she converted to Islam.

Unabated power of madrassas

One of the reasons for the increase in forced conversions is an increase in Islamic religiosity in Pakistan. This has been influenced by the rapid expansion of madrassas – Islamic seminaries – and the unabated power of religious parties and groups across Pakistan in recent years. A survey in 2015 noted there were 28,982 registered madrassas in Pakistan and countless unregistered ones, serving more than 3 million pupils. This number stood at 2,861 in 1988 and 246 in 1947.

In Pakistan, madrassas have played a key role in forced conversion and in Sindh some madrassas have become infamous for facilitating such conversions. For example, Bharchundi Sharif shrine and madrassa and Pir Ayub Jan's madrassa are notorious for promoting and facilitating conversions to Islam.

Curbing forced conversions

So far those Pakistani politicians who have attempted to combat forced conversions have been unsuccessful. In November 2016, the Sindh provincial government passed a bill against forced religious conversion. The bill recommends a five-year punishment for perpetrators, three years for facilitators of forceful religious conversions, and also it makes it a punishable offence to forcibly convert a minor.

But after an outcry by some hardline Muslim religious groups who declared the bill un-Islamic and demanded its withdrawal, the provincial government immediately agreed to review the bill. It has never been ratified.

Forced conversion is, however, covered by provisions in other laws. These include the 2013 act against child marriage in Sindh, and sections of the Pakistan penal code against forced marriage, kidnapping, abducting or inducing into marriage. Yet, implementation of these laws remains limited, largely because of fear a backlash from religious groups.

This means the Government of Pakistan must act decisively to ratify and implement the 2016 law against forced conversions.

14 August 2017

⇨ The above information is reprinted with kind permission from *The Conversation*. Please visit www.theconversation.com for further information.

Harrowing journeys

Key Findings

Adolescents and youth on the move along the Central Mediterranean route (CMR) and the Eastern Mediterranean route (EMR) contend with high levels of abuse, exploitation and discrimination. The risks are much higher on the CMR and are especially acute for some young migrants and refugees:

UNICEF Agenda for Action

UNICEF is calling for a six-point plan to keep refugee and migrant children safe.

Refugee and migrant children are extremely vulnerable to violence and abuse, and to being preyed upon by smugglers and even enslaved by traffickers

UNICEF calls for increasing safe and legal channels for children to migrate and to seek refuge. Cracking down on trafficking, strengthening child protection systems and expanding access to information and assistance can help keep children safe. Children and families should never be returned to face persecution or life-threatening danger in their countries of origin.

Many refugee and migrant children miss out on an education – and many lack access to health care and other essential services

UNICEF calls for increased collective effort by governments, communities and the private sector to provide uprooted children with access to education and health services, and to shelter, nutrition, water and sanitation. A child's migration status should never be a barrier to accessing basic services.

Protracted conflicts, persistent violence and extreme poverty and disadvantage drive millions of children from their homes

UNICEF calls for greater effort to protect children from conflict and to address the root causes of violence and poverty, including by increasing access to education, strengthening health and child protection systems and social safety nets, expanding opportunities for family income and youth employment, and facilitating peaceful conflict resolution and tolerance.

Uprooted children are often victimised by discrimination, xenophobia and stigma – both on their journeys and in their final destinations

Everyone has a part to play in welcoming uprooted children into our cities and communities. UNICEF calls on local leaders, religious groups, NGOs, the media and the private sector to help combat xenophobia and facilitate greater understanding between uprooted children and families with host communities. Governments should also set up stronger measures to combat discrimination and marginalisation in countries of transit and destination.

Adolescents and youth on the move are more vulnerable to trafficking and exploitation than adults

The risks are high for everyone on the CMR – but even higher for adolescents and youth, 77% of whom reported exploitation, compared to 69% of adults 25 and up

On the EMR, 17% of adolescents and youth reported exploitation, compared with 10% of those 25 and older

On the CMR

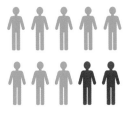

8 of 10 adolescents and youth **reported exploitation**

On the EMR

adolescents and youth face nearly

2x the risk

Source: International Organization for Migration. Displacement Tracking Matrix Flow Monitoring Surveys, January 2016–May 2017

Adolescents and youth from sub-Saharan Africa are at particularly high risk of trafficking and exploitation

On the EMR, the risk is four times higher for sub-Saharan African adolescents and youth – 65% report exploitation, versus 15% of those from other regions

On the CMR, adolescents and youth from sub-Saharan Africa also face considerably higher risks – 83% report exploitation, versus 56% of those from other regions

Anecdotal accounts and qualitative research point to racism as a factor underlying this differential treatment

On the EMR

4x higher risk

for sub-Saharan African adolescents and youth

Source: International Organization for Migration. Displacement Tracking Matrix Flow Monitoring Surveys, January 2016–May 2017

Adolescents and youth travelling alone are more vulnerable to trafficking and exploitation than those in groups

On the EMR, 28% of adolescents and youth travelling alone reported exploitation, compared with 12% of those travelling in groups, whether with family or not

On the CMR, being in a group confers some measure of protection, with 79% of adolescents and youth travelling alone reporting exploitation, compared with 72% of those travelling in groups

On the EMR

travelling alone more than **doubles the risk**
2 x

Source: International Organization for Migration. Displacement Tracking Matrix Flow Monitoring Surveys, January 2016–May 2017

Adolescents with lower levels of education are more vulnerable to trafficking and exploitation

On the EMR, the risks for adolescents with no education are two-thirds higher than those with secondary education – with 23% of the former reporting exploitation, and 14% of the latter

Adolescents with no education face higher risks on the CMR as well, with 90% reporting exploitation, compared with 75% of those with secondary education

On the CMR

9 of 10 adolescents **with no education** reported exploitation

Source: International Organization for Migration. Displacement Tracking Matrix Flow Monitoring Surveys, January 2016–May 2017

Detention is harmful to children's health and well-being – and can undermine their development

UNICEF calls for practical alternatives to detention for all children. Unaccompanied and separated children should be placed in foster care, supervised independent living, or other family- or community-based living arrangements. Children should not be detained in adult facilities.

Children who are travelling alone or who have been separated from their families are more easily preyed upon and more vulnerable to violence and abuse

UNICEF calls for stronger policies to prevent children from being separated from their parents and other family members in transit; and faster procedures to reunite children with their families, including in destination countries. All children need a legal identity and should be registered at birth.

September 2017

⇨ The above information is reprinted with kind permission from UNICEF. Please visit www.unicef.org for further information.

It's time to criminalise the street harassment of children and young people

An article from The Conversation.

THE C⚬NVERSATION

By Rachel Harding, Research Fellow, Nottingham Trent University

'I was walking... to school on my own... all of a sudden this car drove by on the main road and some guy stopped at the red light, wound down his window, stuck his head out and started whistling at me.'

This is an account by an 11-year-old girl of everyday sexism and harassment – and there are countless others like it. But few children or young people know what to do if they are whistled at, beeped at or stared at when they are out and about in public.

'Street harassment' is defined by the activist group Hollaback! as unwelcome comments, gestures and incidents in public, including on public transport. For those who experience it, walking to school, going out with friends, and using the bus, tram, train or tube can become extremely stressful. Children and young people can worry about going out in public. They can even think that something is wrong with them.

What can be done?

There are some, if limited, reporting options for children and young people who experience street harassment. But it is unlikely that such an incident could be successfully prosecuted under the current relevant UK law, the Public Order Act 1986.

And without reliable data, addressing the problem is difficult. Incidents in an area where misogyny is treated by police as a hate crime, such as the English county of Nottinghamshire, can be reported to the police by female children and young people, but this excludes males. It also excludes children and young people who might prefer to categorise their gender as male.

Despite such local anomalies, however, street harassment is not recorded as a crime against young

people in the UK more generally. Sometimes the only option is to write up experiences on the Everyday Sexism Project website – although, again, this tends to be used by females.

To further explore the extent and potential harm of street harassment, five researchers at the Nottingham Centre for Children, Young People and Families, based at Nottingham Trent University, asked secondary school students about street harassment incidents. Although the study is in the early stages it is already providing an insight into the problem.

Anyone, anywhere, at any time

Street harassment can be experienced by anyone, anywhere and at any time. It doesn't seem to matter if young people are wearing school uniform, are out at the weekend, on their own or in a group. Street harassment can also be accompanied by some very mixed, and often negative feelings.

Experiencing street harassment as a child or a young person can have a lasting impact on personal confidence into adulthood and this highlights the potential harm of experiencing incidents when young.

It is important that the harmful impact of street harassment is made known. It might seem trivial to whistle at or call out names to a group of youngsters, or beep a car horn at a young boy and give him the V-sign when he turns around. Yet these and other incidents have the potential to cause confusion, self-doubt, panic, fear and shock.

Managing experiences of street harassment might include talking things through with trusted adults such as parents, family members or teachers. Yet children and young people can worry that nobody will take them seriously, or think their experiences don't matter.

Effectively criminalising street harassment of children and young people could make a real difference. It would send a clear message that street harassment of the young is unacceptable. It would also help protect the next generation.

Children and young people want and need the right to go out in public and not to worry about being harassed. Growing up should not have to include dealing with this pernicious and persistent problem.

11 October 2017

⇨ The above information is reprinted with kind permission from *The Conversation*. Please visit www.theconversation.com for further information.

Key facts

- In 2016, there were significant increases in the number of children seeking asylum from Iran, Iraq and Sudan. Only 30% of unaccompanied children were granted refugee status in 2016. (page 1)

- In 2016, 103 children were locked up in immigration detention compared to 128 in 2015, with 42 under the age of 11. (page 2)

- In 2016, 928 unaccompanied children had their age disputed – almost one-third of all children seeking asylum. (page 1)

- In 2016, 679,000 European national children under the age of 18 resided in the UK. A significant proportion of these children live here long term and around 258,000 (38%) were born in this country. (page 4)

- The UK now ranks among the bottom ten global performers in the arena of improving rights of the child, after it achieved the lowest-possible score across all six available indicators in the domain of Child Rights Environment (CRE). (page 10)

- Last year there were 49,187 children reported as missing from education, according to data obtained from local authorities by the NCB, under freedom of information requests. (page 11)

- All children have the right to be free from all forms of child labour and all workers have the right to safe and healthy workplaces. Globally, 541 million young workers (between the ages of 15 and 24) account for 15 per cent of the world's labour force. (page 13)
  - They sustain up to 40 per cent more non-fatal occupational injuries than do adult workers (workers older than 24) and workplace hazards can even pose a threat to their lives. (page 13)
  - An estimated 152 million children (aged five to 17) around the world are in child labour, of whom 73 million perform work which is hazardous because of its nature or the circumstances in which it is carried out. (page 13)

- The prevalence of child labour is highest in sub-Saharan Africa. In the least-developed countries, around one in four children (ages five to 17) are engaged in labour that is considered detrimental to their health and development. (page 16)

- Sub-Saharan Africa has the largest proportion of child labourers (29 per cent of children aged five to 17 years). In the Middle East and North Africa, fewer than one

in ten (seven per cent) of children in this age group are performing potentially harmful work compared to 11 per cent of children in Latin America and the Caribbean. (page 17)

- In the world's poorest countries, around one in four children are engaged in work that is potentially harmful to their health. (page 17)

- Indian law forbids children below the age of 18 working in mines and other hazardous industries, but many families living in extreme poverty rely on children to boost household incomes which average around 200 rupees (£2.50) a day. (page 19)
  - Campaigners estimate this illegal trade accounts for some 25 per cent of the global production of mica and involves up to 50,000 child workers in India. (page 19)

- Children as young as 14 have been employed to make clothes for some of the most popular names on the UK high street. (page 23)
  - New Look, Sports Direct's Lonsdale brand and H&M have all used factories found to have employed children. (page 23)
  - The legal minimum wage in Myanmar is 3,600 kyat (£2.12) for an eight-hour day – equivalent to 26p an hour. (page 23)
  - The lowest wages of just 13p an hour were found in factories supplying H&M, Karrimor, Muji and Pierre Cardin. The day rate for those workers was £1.06. (page 23)

- Across the globe, levels of child marriage are highest in sub-Saharan Africa, where around four in ten young women were married before age 18, followed by South Asia, where three in ten were married before age 18. Lower levels of child marriage are found in Latin America and the Caribbean (25 per cent), the Middle East and North Africa (17 per cent), and Eastern Europe and Central Asia (11 per cent). (page 25)
  - The prevalence of child marriage is decreasing globally, with the most progress in the past decade seen in South Asia, where a girl's risk of marrying in childhood has dropped by more than a third, from nearly 50 per cent to 30 per cent. (page 25)
  - Around one in four adolescent girls in West and Central Africa are currently married or in union, compared to one in 17 in East Asia and the Pacific. (page 25)

- 80 per cent of forced marriages involving young people based in the UK happen during the summer holidays. (page 32)

- 49,187 children were reported as missing education (CME) at some point in 2016/17. (page 34)

Boycott

A form of activism in which consumers refuse to buy a product or use a service to protest against unethical practices by the manufacturer/provider.

Child exploitation

Child exploitation is a broad term which includes forced or dangerous labour, child trafficking and child prostitution. The term is used to refer to situations where children are abused – physically, verbally or sexually – or when they are submitted to unsatisfactory conditions as part of their forced or voluntary employment.

Child labour

There is no universally-accepted definition of child labour. However, it might generally be said to be work for children that harms or exploits them in some way (physically, mentally, morally or by blocking access to education). According to the International Labour Organization, more than 168 million children worldwide are still in child labour and 85 million at least are subject to its worst forms (are in hazardous work).

Child trafficking

'Trafficking' is not the same as 'people smuggling', where immigrants and asylum seekers pay people to help them enter another country illegally. Victims of trafficking are coerced or deceived by the person arranging their relocation. On arrival in the country of destination, a trafficked child is denied their human rights and forced into exploitation by the trafficker or person into whose control they are delivered.

Child marriage

Where children, often before they have reached puberty, are given to be married – often to a person many years older.

Children's rights

The Convention on the Rights of the Child (CRC) is a human rights treaty which has changed the way that children are viewed and treated since it was established in 1989. The treaty sets out the civil, political, economic, social, health and cultural rights of children.

County lines

County lines is when gangs or organised crime networks use children to sell drugs, often in different counties from where they live. They target vulnerable children and use them to traffic drugs for them. The gangs usually gain a child's trust by offering them money, or gifts and then manipulate them to do as they want to pay off their 'debt'.

Gangs

Gangs are groups of people, often young people who hang around together. They often have a bad reputation as they can sometimes be involved in anti-social or criminal behaviour. Territorial by nature, they are often in violent conflict with gangs from neighbouring areas.

Refugee

A person who has left their native country in order to escape war, persecution or natural disaster. Refugee status is granted in line with the United Nations Convention Relating to the Status of Refugees, which defines which persons are eligible for asylum and which are not: for example, war criminals

Sweatshop

A hazardous or exploitative working environment, where employees may work long hours for very low pay. Employers often violate legal requirements regarding workers' rights, such as minimum pay regulations.

Assignments

Brainstorming

⇨ Brainstorm what you know about Children's rights.

- What is child labour?
- What is an immigrant?
- What is child marriage?

Research

⇨ Choose a country other than your own and do some research into child labour in that country. You should consider the age and gender of the children involved. What type of work might they be involved in? Write a report and share your findings with the rest of your class.

⇨ In small groups, do some research into child refugees. What countries do they come from and where do they end up? Produce a graph to show your findings.

⇨ In pairs, do some research into children who go 'missing' from education. You should consider the reasons this happens, the effect it has upon the child and what could be done to stop this from happening. Write a report which should cover at least one A4 side. Share with the rest of your class.

⇨ Do some research into child marriage. You should consider the reasons why this happens. You should also look at the different countries where this occurs, the ages and gender of the children involved. Produce an infogram to show your findings.

Design

⇨ Image you are working for a children's charity. Design a poster to be displayed in public places such as bus stops and tube stations to highlight the plight of child marriage.

⇨ In groups, design an app for a smartphone that will highlight the issue of forced marriage. Your app should offer help and advice to children who might be at risk. What will your app be called?

⇨ In pairs, design a leaflet which raises awareness of child labour. Include some statistics.

⇨ Choose an article from this book and design an illustration that highlights its key messages.

Oral

⇨ 'Parents who share pictures of their children on social media putting their human rights at risk.' As a class discuss this statement. Have your parents put images of you on the Internet? How did this make you feel? What would you say to a parent who shares images of their child on social media?

⇨ In pairs, discuss the issue of child labour. Write down some of the jobs which children might do. Consider the effect this has on a child. Share your ideas with the rest of your class.

⇨ Imagine that you volunteer for a charity such as ChildLine. You receive a call from a ten-year-old-boy who has health problems. His parents think he is too young to be involved in medical decisions which affect him. What would you advise your caller to do? Discuss your answer in small groups.

⇨ As a class watch the film *Kayleigh's Love Story* which is mentioned on page 35 and warns parents and children of the dangers of online grooming. Have a discussion about this film and the issues it raises.

Reading/writing

⇨ Using the information from this book, write a short paragraph summarising the definition of 'child labour'.

⇨ Imagine you work for a charity which campaigns against child marriage in the UK. Write a blog-post for your charity's website explaining the issues surrounding child marriage and your feelings about this subject.

⇨ Imagine that you are the head master/mistress of a secondary school in the UK. Your are concerned about online grooming and decide to write a letter that will be sent home to parents. Create a draft letter, explaining what online grooming is and the warning signs they should look out for. You should also include advice on where parents can go for help and support if they are worried about their son/daughter.

⇨ Write an article for your school/college newspaper about the harassment of children and young people on our streets. You should include some advice for children who might have been affected.

⇨ Write a summary of the article on page 36 'Forced conversions of Hindu girls in Pakistan make a mockery of its constitution'.

⇨ Read the article 'How high street clothes were made by children in Myanmar for 13p an hour'. Write a letter which is to be sent to high street stores alerting them to the plight of the children involved in making clothes for them. You should try to persuade them to boycott these factories.

Acknowledgements

The publisher is grateful for permission to reproduce the material in this book. While every care has been taken to trace and acknowledge copyright, the publisher tenders its apology for any accidental infringement or where copyright has proved untraceable. The publisher would be pleased to come to a suitable arrangement in any such case with the rightful owner.

Images

All images courtesy of iStock except pages 9, 10, 11, 14, 19, 22 and 39: Pixabay

Icons

Icons on pages 37 and 38 were made by Freepik from www.flaticon.com.

Illustrations

Don Hatcher: pages 24 & 30. Simon Kneebone: pages 12 & 28. Angelo Madrid: pages 4 & 21.

Additional Acknowledgements

With thanks to the Independence team: Shelley Baldry, Danielle Lobban, Jackie Staines and Jan Sunderland.

Tina Brand

Cambridge, October 2018

KT-364-808

Contents

Introduction

CYBERBULLYING is Volume 361 in the **ISSUES** series. The aim of the series is to offer current, diverse information about important issues in our world, from a UK perspective.

ABOUT CYBERBULLYING

Cyberbullying is sadly on the rise, particularly among young people. One in four people in the UK (23%) say they have experienced some form of cyberbullying. It can happen to anyone at any time and usually takes place through social media platforms, but also through online gaming, text messaging and websites. This book looks at the different types of cyberbullying, the impact it has on victims and considers different methods of tackling this problem.

OUR SOURCES

Titles in the **ISSUES** series are designed to function as educational resource books, providing a balanced overview of a specific subject.

The information in our books is comprised of facts, articles and opinions from many different sources, including:

◆ Newspaper reports and opinion pieces

◆ Website factsheets

◆ Magazine and journal articles

◆ Statistics and surveys

◆ Government reports

◆ Literature from special interest groups.

A NOTE ON CRITICAL EVALUATION

Because the information reprinted here is from a number of different sources, readers should bear in mind the origin of the text and whether the source is likely to have a particular bias when presenting information (or when conducting their research). It is hoped that, as you read about the many aspects of the issues explored in this book, you will critically evaluate the information presented.

It is important that you decide whether you are being presented with facts or opinions. Does the writer give a biased or unbiased report? If an opinion is being expressed, do you agree with the writer? Is there potential bias to the 'facts' or statistics behind an article?

ASSIGNMENTS

In the back of this book, you will find a selection of assignments designed to help you engage with the articles you have been reading and to explore your own opinions. Some tasks will take longer than others and there is a mixture of design, writing and research-based activities that you can complete alone or in a group.

FURTHER RESEARCH

At the end of each article we have listed its source and a website that you can visit if you would like to conduct your own research. Please remember to critically evaluate any sources that you consult and consider whether the information you are viewing is accurate and unbiased.

Useful Websites

www.actionforchildren.org.uk

www.bulliesout.com

www.businesscloud.com

www.childline.org.uk

www.counselling-directory.org.uk

www.cyberbcr1me.co.uk

www.ditchthelabel.org

www.gov.uk

www.independent.co.uk

www.mahersconsulting.co.uk

www.manchestereveningnews.co.uk

www.samaritans.org

www.styleofthecitymag.co.uk

www.telegraph.co.uk

www.theconversation.com

www.thecourier.co.uk

www.theguardian.com

www.themckeownclinic.co.uk

www.warwick.ac.uk

www.worldeconomicforum.com

www.yougov.co.uk

www.youngminds.org.uk

Cyberbullying

Editor: Tracy Biram

Volume 361

Independence Educational Publishers

First published by Independence Educational Publishers

The Studio, High Green

Great Shelford

Cambridge CB22 5EG

England

© Independence 2019

ISBN-13: 978 1 86168 817 0

Printed in Great Britain

Zenith Print Group

What is cyberbullying?

Cyberbullying can be a persistent, hard to spot form of bullying that feels like it knows no boundaries. Unlike other types of bullying, it can happen anytime, anywhere – even in the safety of your own home.

In this modern, digital age, we are spending more and more time online. Whether it's using a smartphone to scroll through social media, catching up with our favourite YouTube channels on a tablet, or chatting with friends through Facebook groups on our PCs. But we're not the only ones spending more time than ever before living our lives digitally – our children are too.

Is your child or teen being cyberbullied?

YoungMinds' *Safety Net Report* looked into the impact of cyberbullying on children's mental health. Through speaking to young people, they discovered almost 30% spend more than four hours each day browsing social media, with 44% admitting to three or more hours per day. When asked, 61% admitted to creating their first social media account before the age of 12 (despite guidelines requiring users to be 13 or older).

Children and teens are not only spending more time living their lives online than any previous generation, but they are also finding their digital lives affect their relationships and sense of self-worth in real life. 62% of young people reported that social media had impacted their friendships, with a further 38% saying it had a negative impact on how they feel about themselves.

For young women and girls, almost one in two (46%) found that social media had, and continued to, negatively impact their self-esteem.

Social media alone can have a huge impact on the well-being and sense of self-worth for younger users. When cyberbullying comes into play, it can have an even more damaging impact. Those who took part in the YoungMinds report spoke of a perceived lack of consequences for those who they saw as engaging in bullying behaviour online.

Many expressed concerns that the responsibility fell to those who were being bullied to act first, rather than the platforms or communities as a whole standing up to protect and defend users. From the perspective of many young people, those who they saw bullying others online faced few (if any) consequences from their actions.

Also known as digital bullying, cyberbullying encompasses any form of bullying behaviour that takes place online, through smartphones, tablets or computers. It can be through mean private or public messages, posts, photographs or groups, via social media, networking apps, gaming sites, chat rooms or video sharing platforms. Unlike bullying in person, online bullying can happen anytime, anywhere. This can leave the victims feeling on edge and under attack at all times, as they never know when or where the next message will come.

YoungMinds and The Children's Society spoke to over 1,000 young people aged 11–25 to get a greater idea of the scope of cyberbullying. Almost half (47%) reported an experience with threatening, intimidating, or nasty messages through social media, email or text, with 32% saying that their personal, private or embarrassing information was shared publicly by their bullies. 39% felt they had been personally bullied online, with 27% saying it had happened within the last year. 60% had seen others being harassed or bullied online. Over half (56%) had been deliberately excluded from conversations, groups, games and activities online by peers. When asked what had happened with their cyberbullying experience, 30% experienced persistent messages despite asking their bully to stop.

While offline bullying still remains more prominent (with 49% of young people reporting experiences with bullying), the relentless nature of cyberbullying, combined with the potential to reach a larger audience, the long-lasting and far-reaching effects mean that digital bullying can escalate more quickly than we may realise.

For young people who are already experiencing mental ill health, research has found that they are three times more likely to have been bullied online within the past year.

Cyberbullies may directly harass their target online, or may do so by spreading fake or damaging information, gossip or rumours publically or amongst shared friends and acquaintances online. Cyberbullying can encompass digital stalking, exclusion, blackmail, abusive comments, inappropriate tagging or hashtags, flaming, impersonation and many other behaviours.

It is vital to make sure that all young people understand that, just as with in-person experiences, there is no such thing as an innocent bystander when it comes to bullying. If they see someone being bullied or see something that makes them feel uncomfortable, reporting it to the site or app is important. Ignoring it or scrolling past may seem easier, but the person who is being bullied may need help and support to stop what is happening and reinforce the idea that it's never OK to bully someone.

No form of bullying should be seen as less damaging or 'not as bad' as another. Each can have a lasting, negative impact on the person's mental, physical and/or emotional wellbeing. Making sure that young people understand this and feel able to seek help and support is crucial.

The signs of cyberbullying

Experiencing bullying can feel overwhelming, distressing and embarrassing. Many young people may not feel comfortable and confident in seeking support or may be unsure of where they can go to find help. Cyberbullying can have a serious impact on those who are targeted. It can be a constant source of worry, feeling relentless. When victims

feel cornered or unable to find vital help and support, there can be extreme consequences, including an increase in self-harming behaviours or suicide.

If you are concerned about a child, young person or loved one, there are many warning signs you can look out for, These can include:

◆ low or changing levels of self-esteem or confidence

◆ a sudden withdrawal from family, friends or loved ones

◆ increased time or desire to be left alone

◆ a new or increased reluctance to leave family or friends near their mobile or laptop etc.

◆ an increased desire and range of excuses to stay home from school, college or clubs

◆ decreased time spent with friends or being excluded from social events/activities

◆ a change in their personality (increased anger, appearing withdrawn, anxious or depressed)

◆ weight loss, gain, or an increased desire to change their appearance to 'fit in'

◆ changes in what they wear that are unusual or out of season

◆ self-harming behaviours.

How can you help?

Young people who initially seek help through the online platforms where they are experiencing (or witnessing) cyberbullying may become disillusioned and reluctant to speak out.

When surveyed, 83% of young people felt social media companies should be doing more to tackle cyberbullying, with many expressing concerns that the current systems in place have:

◆ unclear reporting systems

◆ delayed or no responses

◆ an overall lack of support for those who report online bullying

◆ unclear communication about rights, responsibilities, guidelines and safety features.

Letting your child or teen know that you are there for them, that people love, care and want to support them is the first step. Reinforce the idea that no-one deserves to be treated this way, and they have done nothing wrong. It's important to make sure that they understand that help is available, and people are available to listen.

Talk to them

Encourage them to talk with you, or if they may feel more comfortable, with a teacher, another loved one, or a close family friend. Speaking to a teacher can be a good way to set up a safe place they are able to go to at school if things get too much for them, as well as to keep an eye out for any further signs that bullying may be taking place on school grounds.

Record evidence

Take screenshots of the cyberbullying and save them for your record. This can help when reporting incidents to the relevant social media networks, apps or platforms, as you will have a collection of proof if the bully or bullies attempt to remove or delete any of their messages or photographs.

Write down thoughts and worries

Encourage the young person to keep a journal. This can provide a private, safe space to write down their thoughts and feelings. By bottling things up and not expressing how the experience is making them feel, it can risk them feeling worse or cause them to constantly dwell on their negative thoughts. Through writing things down, they may be better able to articulate themselves, understand their emotions, and even feel more able to speak to someone.

Speak to the school

Get (and keep) the school involved. Whether things are taking place on school grounds or not, they may be able to help. Make sure to put everything down in writing, where possible, so you can have a formal record of what happens and ensure that everybody is on the same page. Ask if the school or college has a counselling service or any further support your child or teen can access. Speaking to an impartial, outside expert can be easier for some young people as they may not be as worried what they will think or how they may react.

Seek further support

If you are unable to access counselling through their school or college, many charities offer free one-to-one services online and in person. Seeing a counsellor privately can also be another option. Counselling can provide a safe space for young people to discuss their worries and concerns. While a counsellor won't be able to stop bullies' behaviour, they may be able to help the young person to process their feelings, deal with any anger, frustration or low self-esteem that may stem from being bullied. They may also be able to help them to process what has happened, and gain an insight into why bullies act the way they do.

If you're concerned about their safety or any other signs, seek advice from your GP. They may be able to refer you to specialist CAMHS services in your local area.

Cyberbullying

Statistics from the Department of Education document: Bullying in England, April 2013 to March 2018. Analysis on 10 to 15 year olds from the ONS Crime Survey for England and Wales.

In the year ending March 2018, 7% of children said that they had experienced cyberbullying. There has been no significant change in this figure from previous years (see below).

Percentage experiencing cyber bullying in the previous 12 months

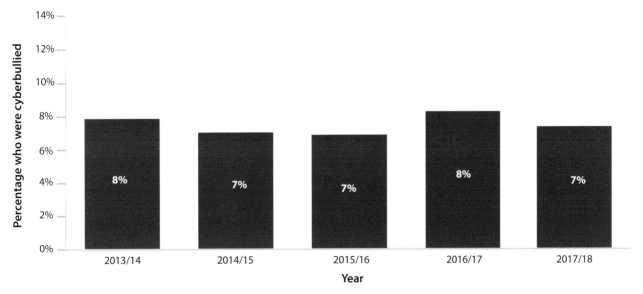

Note: Percentages show the number of children who answered 'Yes' as a proportion of all children who answered including those who answered 'Don't know' (approx 2% per year) and 'Don't want to answer' (approx 1% per year).
Charts are produced using unrounded data but labelled to the nearest whole percentage for ease of reading.

In the year ending March 2018, girls were more likely than boys to have experienced cyberbullying (9% compared to 5%) – this is a statistically significant difference. Similar patterns were seen in previous years (see below)

Percentage experiencing cyberbullying by gender

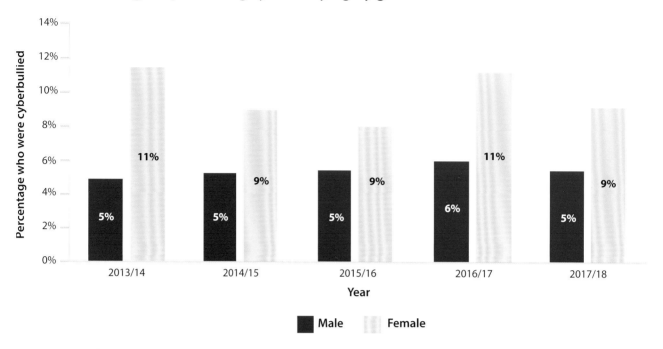

Note: Charts are produced using unrounded data but labelled to the nearest whole percentage for ease of reading.

Experience of cyberbullying did not vary significantly by age (see below).

Percentage experiencing cyberbullying by age

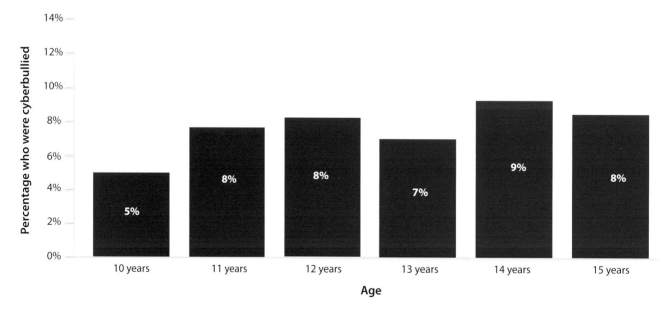

Note: Data for April 2013 to March 2018 combined.
Charts are produced using unrounded data but labelled to the nearest whole percentage for ease of reading.

Quarter of children experienced cyberbullying in past year, study finds

'It's vital that young users can reap the benefits of going online without being exposed to unacceptable harm.'

By Sabrina Barr

Around one in four children have experienced a form of online abuse in the past 12 months, new research has revealed.

Ofcom, the UK's communications regulator, conducted a study with the Information Commissioner's Office (ICO) to identify concerns the nation has about using the Internet.

Their findings, which were published in Ofcom's first annual *Online Nation* report, showed that 23% of children have been cyberbullied in the last year, while 39% have been subjected to offensive language online.

Just under one in three children received unwelcome friend requests, while a fifth experienced trolling.

Ofcom and ICO carried out the study by analysing responses from a quantitative study of 2,047 adult Internet users and 1,001 children aged between 12 and 15.

Almost 80% of the children said they had a 'potentially harmful online experience' in the past year.

The majority of these harmful online experiences – 24% – occurred on Facebook, with 12% taking place on Instagram and 8% on Snapchat.

Tony Stower, head of child safety online at the NSPCC, said that it's 'vital' for young Internet users to 'reap the benefits of going online without being exposed to unacceptable harm'.

'It is blatantly clear that, left to their own devices, tech firms will not protect young users and, once again, we urge the government to move quickly in bringing in robust new laws with tough sanctions for tech firms that fail to keep children safe,' Stower said.

In addition to the extent to which children experience cyberbullying online, the study also delved into the amount of time adults spend browsing the Internet on a daily basis. The report stated that adults spent an average of three hours and 15 minutes online every day in the past year, an 11-minute increase to the average amount of time spent online in 2017.

Several factors for this increase included the high speed of the Internet, the use of social media platforms such as Facebook and the widespread use of smartphones.

The study revealed that Facebook users spend approximately 23 minutes on the site on a daily basis, equating to just under six days a year.

Seven in ten of the adults surveyed said they think social media platforms should be better regulated.

However, 59% of the adults expressed their belief that the benefits of going online outweigh the negatives, with 61% of the children agreeing with this point of view.

'As most of us spend more time than ever online, we're increasingly worried about harmful content – and also more likely to come across it,' said Yih-Choung Teh, group director of strategy and research at Ofcom.

'For most people, those risks are still outweighed by the huge benefits of the Internet.'

The Ofcom group director added that free speech is 'one of the internet's great strengths'.

30 May 2019

Types of cyberbullying

Infographic adapted from cybercr1me.co.uk.

Harassment
Harassment involves sending offensive, insulting or humiliating online comments or messages, or being offensive on gaming sites.

Flaming
Flaming involves using extremely offensive language in order to get into online arguments or fights.

Denigration
Denigration is when someone sends fake information or photos about another which is damaging and untrue

Impersonation
Impersonation involves hacking or faking another's email or social networking account to use their online identity to post offensive material online.

Outing & trickery
When someone shares personal information about another or tricks someone into sharing secrets, before forwarding it onto others.

Cyber stalking
Repeatedly sending threatening, harassing and intimidating messages, or engaging in online activity by making a person afraid for their safety.

Exclusion
Intentionally leaving someone out of a group such as group messaging, online apps and gaming sites.

Trolling
Trolling is the deliberate act of provoking a response by using insults or bad language on forums and social networking sites.

Catfishing
Like impersonation, catfishing involves stealing anothers online identity to pose as them and deceive others.

The above information is reprinted with kind permission from Cybercrime Services.
© Cybercrime Services 2019

www.cybercr1me.co.uk

Cyberbullying afflicts quarter of Brits

18-to 24-year-olds are the most likely group to be bullied online, but the unpleasant practice affects Britons of every age – and leads to confidence problems in real-life conversations.

By Victoria Waldersee

A number of recent campaigns have tackled cyberbullying among children. But new YouGov research reveals that it also affects adults, ranging from outright abuse to cyberstalking and social exclusion.

One in eight Britons have been harassed online

One in four Britons (23%) say they have experienced some form of cyberbullying before. Of these, one in ten (10%) have experienced it in the last fortnight alone. Another one in six (15%) say it's happened to them in the last six months, while half (52%) of cyberbullying victims said the last time it happened was over a year ago.

The most common form of cyberbullying is harassment, when a person sends abusive or hateful messages. One in eight Brits (13%) say this has happened to them before. Flaming is when someone uses offensive language in a deliberate attempt to get into a fight – something which has been experienced by one in eleven (9%) Britons online.

Like any other social space, people can bully you online simply by excluding you. One in 14 (7%) Brits feel this has happened to them online.

One in 20 (5%) have been cyberstalked, where someone sends messages repeatedly that make you afraid for your safety.

One in 14 (7%) have had someone spread fake and potentially damaging information about them online, and 4% say someone has impersonated them online and messaged a third party.

Harassment is the most common form of cyberbullying
Which, if any, of the following forms of cyberbullying have you ever experienced online?
Please select all that apply. % Excluding 'Don't know' (3%), 'Other' (1%), and 'Prefer not to say' (1%)

Not applicable – I have never experienced any form of cyberbullying	73
Harrassment: sending you offensive, rude, insulting messages and/or being abusive online	13
Flaming: using extremely offensive language in a deliberate attempt to get into an argument or fight	9
Denigration: someone spreading information about you that is fake, damaging or untrue	7
Exclusion: someone intentionally leaving you out of online group situations like messaging or gaming sites	7
Cyberstalking: someone repeatedly sending messages to you that make you afraid for your safety	5
Impersonation: someone using your online identity and sending material to others	4
Outing/Trickery: someone sharing your personal information such as data or photos of you	3
Revenge porn: someone uploading intimate photos of you without your permission	2

18-to 24-year-olds most likely to experience cyberbullying

Cyberbullying is significantly more common among young people - just four in ten 18- to 24-year-olds (43%) say they've never experienced any of the above forms of cyberbullying, leaving half of 18- to 24-year-olds (52%) who have (the remaining respondents said 'don't know' or 'prefer not to say').

By comparison, nine out of ten (87%) of those aged 55 and above say they've never experienced any of the listed forms of cyberbullying.

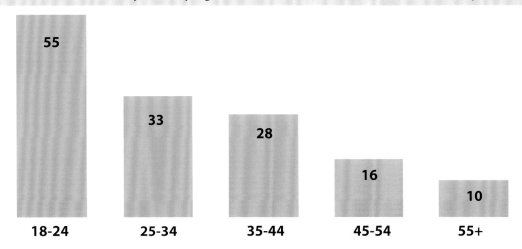

18-to-24 year olds more than five times as likely as those aged 55 and above to say they have experienced cyberbullying
Which, if any, of the following forms of cyberbullying have you ever experienced online? % who selected at least one form of cyberbullying and did NOT select 'other', 'don't know' or 'prefer not to say'

18-24	25-34	35-44	45-54	55+
55	33	28	16	10

Most of those who reported cyberbullying say it happened on Facebook (56%). One in six (15%) say it has happened to them on Twitter. Around one in 14 (7%) have been bullied on YouTube, or Snapchat (6%).

You're most likely to be bullied online by a total stranger

Our research reveals that you're more likely to be cyberbullied by a total stranger. Four in ten (44%) of those who've experienced it say it came from someone they'd never spoken to online or in person before. This is particularly common among those aged 55 and above (56%).

You are most likely to be 'cyberbullied' by a total stranger
Thinking about any experiences you have had of cyberbullying... Which, if any, of the following people have you ever experienced cyberbullying from? Select all that apply. % of people who have experienced cyberbullying

A total stranger who I had never spoken to before online or in person	44
An acquaintance that I have met online but not in person	19
A friend that I am not particularly close to	18
An acquaintance that I have met in person but do not know well	13
A close friend or family member (excluding a current/previous partner)	11
A former partner/someone I once dated	9
A colleague	6
A current partner (i.e. my current partner at the time of the cyberbullying	3
Don't know/can't recall	12
Other	5
Prefer not to say	4

One in five (19%) victims say it was an acquaintance they'd met online, but not in person, while one in ten (11%) say it was a close friend or family member.

One in 30 (3%) say the perpetrator was their current partner, and three times as many (9%) have been cyberbullied by an ex.

Some have experienced cyberbullying from a person they know but not well – one in five (18%) say it was a friend they aren't particularly close to, and one in eight (13%) say it was an acquaintance they've met in person but don't know well – though both these figures are significantly higher among 18- to-24-year olds (30% and 22%, respectively).

The majority of cyberbullying victims did not report the incident to the website it happened on

Just over half (53%) of those who've experienced cyberbullying have never reported the incident to the website or service in question.

One in eight (12%) always reported it, while just over one in six (17%) reported only occasionally.

Women are ten percentage points more likely than men to say they've never reported an incident (58% versus 48%).

Among those who chose not to report, half (50%) said it was because they didn't think it would make any difference. A quarter (24%) thought they wouldn't be taken seriously, and around one in eight didn't understand (12%) or trust (13%) the process.

Cyberbullying affects confidence in real-life discussions

A third (29%) of people who've experienced cyberbullying say they carried on with life as normal, with no particular consequences. But one in five (22%) say it caused them to engage less on the website or social media platform.

Shockingly, one in four (23%) 18- to-24-year olds who've experienced cyberbullying say they have less confidence engaging in real-life discussions as a result of their experience online – compared to one in seven (14%) of cyberbullying victims across all age groups.

One in five who've been cyberbullied say their experience has led them to feel less confident in real-life discussions
Which, if any, of the following things have you ever experienced as as result of being cyberbullied? % Excluding those who said 'not applicable' – nothing in particular has happened to me as a result of being cyberbullied (29%), 'Don't know' (9%), and 'Prefer not to say' (4%)

I engaged less on the website/social media platform than I used to	22
I removed myself from the website/social media platform for a period of time but have since returned	14
I had less confidence in engaging in real-life discussions as a result of my experience online	14
I struggled to sleep	11
I became more likely to speak out it I think someone else is being bullied online	11
I removed myself permanently from the website/ social media platform	8
I felt stronger as a reuslt of having been through the experience	8
I had an increased faith in social media communities (i.e. people on social media platforms) because people stood up for me	4
I had an increased faith in the website/social media platform in question because of the way they responded	2
Other	9

One in seven (14%) people removed themselves entirely from the website for a period, but have since returned, while one in twelve (8%) removed themselves permanently from it. One in nine (11%) say they struggled to sleep because of what happened.

Still, some reported silver linings to their experience: one in nine (11%) say they are now more likely to speak out if they think someone else is being bullied online, and just under one in twenty (4%) feel their faith in social media communities has increased because others stood up for them.

28 April 2019

www.yougov.co.uk

Cyberbullying rarely occurs in isolation, research finds

- ◆ Cyberbullying doesn't create large numbers of new victims, says University of Warwick researchers
- ◆ Most bullying is face-to-face – with cyberbullying used as a modern tool to supplement traditional forms
- ◆ 29% of UK teenagers reported being bullied – only 1% were victims of cyberbullying alone
- ◆ Bullying intervention strategies should focus on traditional bullying as well as cyberbullying

Cyberbullying is mostly an extension of playground bullying – and doesn't create large numbers of new victims – according to research from the University of Warwick.

Professor Dieter Wolke in the Department of Psychology finds that although cyberbullying is prevalent and harmful, it is a modern tool used to harm victims already bullied by traditional, face-to-face means.

In a study of almost 3,000 pupils aged 11–16 from UK secondary schools, 29 per cent reported being bullied, but one per cent of adolescents were victims of cyberbullying alone.

During the survey, pupils completed the Bullying and Friendship Interview, which has been used in numerous studies to assess bullying and victimisation.

They were asked about direct victimisation (e.g., 'been hit/beaten up' or 'called bad/nasty names'); relational victimisation (e.g. 'had nasty lies/rumours spread about you'); and cyber-victimisation (e.g. 'had rumours spread about you online', 'had embarrassing pictures posted online without permission' or 'got threatening or aggressive emails, instant messages, text messages or tweets').

All the teenagers who reported being bullied in any form had lower self-esteem, and more behavioural difficulties than non-victims.

However, those who were bullied by multiple means – direct victimisation, relational victimisation and cyber-victimisation combined – demonstrated the lowest self-esteem and the most emotional and behavioural problems.

The study finds that cyberbullying is 'another tool in the toolbox' for traditional bullying, but doesn't create many unique online victims.

As a result, Professor Wolke argues that public health strategies to prevent bullying overall should still mainly focus on combating traditional, face-to-face bullying – as that is the root cause of the vast majority of cyberbullying.

Professor Wolke comments:

'Bullying is a way to gain power and peer acceptance, being the 'cool' kid in class. Thus, cyberbullying is another tool that is directed towards peers that the bully knows, and bullies, at school.

'Any bullying prevention and intervention still needs to be primarily directed at combatting traditional bullying while considering cyberbullying as an extension that reaches victims outside the school gate and 24/7.'

6 March 2017

Girls more likely to be bullied than boys, English schools survey finds

Government study finds violent bullying down, cyberbullying and social exclusion up.

By Richard Adams

Girls are much more likely than boys to be bullied at school, with almost twice as many on the receiving end of cyberbullying and social exclusion by other pupils, according to a government study.

The figures from a survey of 10,000 pupils at schools in England in year 11 – children aged 15 or 16 – revealed a decline in reports of bullying overall and particularly in incidents of violent bullying, which mainly affects boys.

But girls reported a rise in bullying, with more than one in three telling researchers they had been affected in the previous year, while only about one in four boys said they had been victims of bullying in any form.

The report published by the Department for Education said the overall trends around bullying in schools were 'broadly positive', with the rate of bullying reported falling from 37% of pupils in year 10 to 30% for the same cohort 12 months later in year 11.

Incidents of bullying were slightly lower compared with a similar study in 2006, forms of violent bullying were lower than a decade before – with threats of violence reported by pupils down from 14% to 10%, and actual violence down from 10% to 6%.

'While violent forms of bullying have declined significantly, name calling and social exclusion have increased since 2006. The success in reducing violent bullying shows what can be achieved; the challenge is to replicate this success across all forms of bullying,' the report concluded.

Tom Bennett, an adviser to the DfE on behaviour policies and teacher training, said the overall reduction was to be welcomed but warned that bullying was 'an evergreen problem' when students were competing for attention and status.

'It's perhaps unsurprising to see boys as more likely to experience violence, and girls to be the victims of social exclusion,' he said. 'The latter is less visible, and the bruises it leaves can be intangible.

'The problem this causes is that it means such bullying can fall below the radar, and schools need to be proactive in both creating cultures where students feel safe and valued, and also respond accurately and quickly to allegations.

'The complexity of who is the bully and who is the bullied also often makes policing this sphere unbelievably difficult, and the inexorable move of such activities online presents huge challenges to even the most concerned teacher.'

The data comes from the third wave of a longitudinal study of young people in England managed by the DfE, with the surveys conducted in 2015 and 2014. The longer-term comparison was with a similar survey taken in 2006.

Cyberbullying did not feature in the 2006 version, but 10% of the 15- and 16-year-olds reported being affected in the most recent study.

For girls the most common form of bullying was name calling and social exclusion, with both types having increased significantly since 2006. But the rise occurred entirely for girls, with boys reporting no increase in either types of bullying. While one in five girls reported being a victim of social exclusion, fewer than one in ten boys did.

Disabled children and children with special needs also reported much higher incidents of bullying than other pupils.

The survey results also showed that pupils who were victims of bullying received lower GCSE results than their peers who hadn't been bullied, by the equivalent of two grades in one GCSE exam.

But the authors of the research said it was 'important to note that this simple correlation does not demonstrate causation between bullying and lower GCSE performance; there are likely to be many other factors involved'.

13 June 2018

The psychology of an online troll

Attack of the Keyboard Warrior.

Blogpost by Steve McKeown

You're on your favourite social media platform and an idea springs to mind that you want to post, or you decide to share someone else's post. To you, your post is tepid, inoffensive and polite. You wonder if anyone will like the post, or even bother to comment on it.

After logging off to complete your day, you settle down in the evening and decide to see if anyone noticed your post. You are pleasantly surprised that your post has received seven likes and 15 comments. You click on the comments and your heart sinks. Amongst the jolly banter from friends are hidden a couple of nasty, even sinister messages about your post. What alarms you aside from the content of the messages is that you don't know the people commenting. You shudder and feel as though you are being stalked.

Say hello to the Keyboard Warrior, often referred to as a troll or hater. Your mind wonders why they would type such poison, especially when they don't know you and have never met you. Your evening is ruined. You toss and turn in bed, then awaken to a new day, put the kettle on and suddenly your mind tracks back to yesterday's post's reaction. Your mood darkens and you have a miserable start to the day.

Such 'trolling' has become commonplace in recent years. Social media has become a safe haven for haters. Being anonymous, or hiding safely behind the screen in their bedrooms offers protection for people to say whatever they want, be it constructive or abusive.

Arguably celebrities suffer more than most, because they are an easy target, their faces being plastered everywhere, their comments being potentially controversial, their wealth often seen by the haters as something to be envious of, as opposed to aspirational. They often suffer a virtual social flogging or stoning.

So what constitutes a troll? Who are they, how are they wired, what is their psychology, what drives their behaviour?

They do not all fit into one particular box. However, they all demonstrate similar tactics.

Often, they can be people who have been abused or are suffering abuse themselves.

Feeling helpless, they project their inner misery onto others in the form of written abuse. They may suffer from an identity issue, an insecurity about their own identity.

Their way of coping with this crisis or inner turmoil is to belittle others, which gives them a self-satisfied feeling of justification, that their lives mean something more than

their own poor image of themselves. They feel they have no control over their own lives and seek to control others via their belittling behaviour. These types feel no remorse and rarely stop. This may be a pattern for their entire lives.

In a study conducted by Canadian researchers involving 1,215 people, they came to the conclusion that trolling can be clearly linked with the 'Dark Tetrad' of personality traits, which are narcissism, Machiavellianism, psychopathy and sadism. In fact, the results were so significant, they stated: '… the associations between sadism and GAIT (Global Assessment of Internet Trolling) scores were so strong that it might be said that online trolls are prototypical everyday sadists.'

With such traits, trolls will likely exhibit such tactics away from their safe chair behind the screen. They may bully their own families and friends, exhibit aggressive or passive aggressive behaviour and be unpleasant to people in general. They may be the type to drive aggressively. They are unlikely to feel they have personality flaws and will look to blame negative feedback from others on those who object to their behaviour. Research indicates that bullies actually have excellent self-esteem, which ties in with the Dark Tetrad. 'Bullies usually have a sense of entitlement and superiority over others, and lack compassion, impulse control and social skills.'

However, not all trolls are psychopaths or bullies! Deindividuation (temporary identity loss and anonymity) could bring out the worst in some people by lifting moral constraints and inhibitions. It has been seen in gaming, role-playing and hooliganism, 'fuelling dissent and triggering

abrasive reactions'. The reward for the hater is a perceived enhanced status, as they are likely to be less effective in attracting attention in the real world.

Some may be motivated by negative social rewards, like creating mayhem, something that may keep them coming back for more. Due to the addictive nature of rewards, there may be an addictive element to trolling. If the effects upon us of this continual barrage are left to fester, they could damage our own self-esteem.

We don't need to tolerate or suffer at the hands of these Keyboard Warriors. There are plenty of self-protection methods we can apply, for example gaining resilience by building an internal Locus of Control. In essence, this means we own a sense of control over our lives, rather than externalising control, thus giving it to other people, other things such as fate, hope, etc. By nurturing an internal Locus of Control, we are able to laugh at trolling comments, ignore them or indeed feel pity for the troll. Think that this behaviour is likely common to the rest of their lives, something that has damaged or destroyed most of their relationships.

Being unable to control Keyboard Warriors, we can control the way we feel about them: remember that they do not know us personally and therefore such hateful comments are not personal.

5 December 2018

Cyberbullying in the workplace: 'I became paranoid'

Technology has blurred the line between professional and personal life, giving bullies more ways to reach their victims.

By Sarah Shearman

Technology has dramatically changed the way we work, allowing people to work remotely and connecting colleagues around the world. But there is a darker side to these new technological advances, as many workers are finding out.

Shortly after starting a new job at a PR firm in London, Clare* found herself a victim of cyberbullying at work. 'My colleagues would be emailing or texting each other while in the same room and then smirking and laughing at each other. This escalated to one of them 'accidentally' sending me emails that contained insults about me and then feigning innocence and saying it wasn't about me and he didn't know why I'd got the email.'

Clare's colleagues also tried to damage her reputation with her boss and contacts outside of the business. 'They would purposely tell me the wrong time to arrive at events, so they could then tell the boss I was late. They also repeatedly didn't copy me into other email communications so I was left in the dark about what was going on at work, then email me asking me to follow up with something I had no idea about,' she says.

'I began to dread going into work and became paranoid, wondering what every email they sent was saying and if it was about me. I felt constantly anxious and close to tears, and was reminded of the misery of school bullying,' she says.

Cyberbullying is often associated with teenagers and schools, but it is increasingly common in workplaces. 'Adult cyberbullying in the workplace can be more subtle, but is equally distressing.

The outcomes are often the same – to humiliate, undermine and distress the person being targeted,' says Dan Raisbeck, co-founder of anti-cyberbullying charity The Cybersmile Foundation.

Clare believes that working in a small company meant she did not receive adequate support when she raised the issue with her boss. So after six months she decided to leave. 'There is a feeling that the bullies have 'won' if you're the one that ends up quitting,' she says. "But I had to weigh up whether taking the moral high ground and refusing to be beaten was worth the impact it was having on my mental health.'

Victims of bullying are often told to toughen up and just ignore the behaviour. But with technology generating an always-on work culture, and blurring the boundaries between personal and professional lives, bullies have new ways to infiltrate their victim's life outside office hours.

Fiona* also found herself subject of insulting emails sent between her former team-mates at the digital marketing agency where she worked in Manchester. This bullying, which took place over the course of a year and got worse when she was promoted, extended beyond the physical realm of the office, spilling into her personal life. 'When I would put something on Instagram, they would screenshot it and mock it. Even when I was away from the office or on holiday, I'd think about what I would post and second guess myself.' She was afraid that blocking them on social networks would make matters worse.

'I'm normally a very happy and confident person. It really destroyed my confidence for a bit and made me meeker,' she says.

Cyberbullying often inspires a 'gang/pack mentality' in workplaces, leaving the victim feeling very isolated, says Emma Kenny, psychologist and founder of wellbeing site Make Your Switch. 'It can almost feel like stalking – as if people know something about your life, true or untrue,' she says.

Protecting employees

The fluidity between work and home presents a challenge for employers who want to stamp out bullying behaviour – especially as they increasingly use social media tools themselves for employee engagement. Since employers have a duty of care to their employees, is it their responsibility to take action if the bullying between co-workers takes place outside of the office on personal computers and devices?

The law is still catching up in this area, but it is possible for employers to discipline employees and even fire them for their behaviour and activities outside of work, says Anna

Byford, senior employment lawyer at Kemp Little, a law firm that specialises in technology and digital media.

'What is particularly challenging for employers – assuming they are good ones trying to create a culture where [bullying] is not acceptable – is that there is every chance they won't know about it, so their ability to police it is quite limited,' she says.

Having well-drafted company policies, which spell out that this behaviour will be considered a disciplinary offence, irrespective of whether it occurs outside or inside of the office, is helpful here, says Byford. More broadly, employers should be thinking about creating procedures and training to ensure they have a culture able to deal with bullying, she says. Fiona has since found a new job at a larger, global company, where she says such policies are in place. She believes that if her previous employer monitored communications between staff, the issue would have been picked up and sorted out earlier. 'We were always told that we were being monitored, but evidently we weren't.'

How much companies can monitor their employees is a grey area, however. 'Most employers aren't monitoring everything their employees do because that's very difficult to justify,' says Byford. 'But when it comes to cyberbullying, they may be able to justify it, provided it is proportionate – and their position is a lot stronger if they have informed employees in a policy in their contract that they may monitor email correspondence where they suspect wrongdoing.'

Since offending digital communications can be saved and stored, it is arguably easier for victims to collect evidence of cyberbullying themselves. Yet there is always the risk that digital communications might be misconstrued or interpreted differently, too – which bullies could use to justify their behaviour. Taking note of incidents related to the cyberbullying – such as being passed over for a pay rise or promotion – can be helpful in these circumstances, says Byford.

Since being cyberbullied, Fiona is wary of friendships in the workplace and makes a point of stepping away from the computer and building face-to-face relationships with colleagues and avoiding cliques. 'People hide behind their keyboards. I make sure it's not all the same people who go to lunch together, not always the same people who work together on a project, and I make sure I have open conversations, rather than constant email threads.'

*Some names have been changed

30 March 2017

Nine things to think about before posting something negative online

When shade can be thrown in any comments section, and subtweeting someone seems to be the only way to get stuff off your chest, it can seem like being negative online is a pretty common thing. The thing is, a lot of people don't realise that the kind of negativity that they take part in online can actually be called cyberbullying, and can get serious.

One in three people have been cyberbullied at some point in their lifetimes, and we are not into that. We do know though that sometimes it can feel easy to do it, like it's the only way to express yourself, or like it won't matter. That's why we have come up with a little checklist of things to think about before you post something negative online, so that hopefully next time you think about doing it, you will make a cup of tea instead.

1) Why are you posting it?

Have a think about why you are posting it. Is it to take part in healthy debate and conversation or is it just to hurt someone's feelings? A good idea is to write a list of as many reasons as you can think of why you feel the need to do it, and a list of reasons why you shouldn't. Seeing it all written down might give you a bit of perspective on the situation. Plus, the chances are, you won't be able to come up with that many reasons why you should.

2) How are you saying it?

We can all say stuff from time to time that comes across badly when we didn't mean it to. Especially because we can't really convey tone on the internet, and a lot of sarcasm, irony or even humour may get lost and taken the wrong way. Before tapping that send button it's always a good shout to give your comment or message a read through and make sure you aren't accidentally saying something you don't mean.

3) Can the person you are posting it to/about do anything about it?

Is it a conversation that they can be a part of, offer their side of the story or defend themselves against any allegations that might get made? Imagine if you heard that all this stuff was being said against you behind your back, and you had no way of trying to solve the situation and make things right. It would totally suck, and would probably feel pretty unfair.

4) Would you say it to their face?

A big reason why we all find it easy to say negative stuff online is because we can do it from behind a screen, and it is way easier to type insults or rumours than it is to actually say them out loud.

Always think if you would feel comfortable saying something to someone's face before typing it out on your phone and hitting send.

Plus, even though it might seem like it can be easy to be anonymous on social media, everything that you put out there is staying there until you take it down for the most part, and there is absolutely no guarantee it will stay anonymous forever. There is always going to be the possibility that you get in trouble for it somewhere down the line, or affect your career, relationships, school records and in the most serious of cases, could land you in trouble with the law. Not chill, huh?

5) How do you feel right now?

If you are thinking about saying something mean or negative online to or about someone, it might be a good idea to check in with yourself first. It might be that there is something going on with you that you didn't even realise was making you want to behave this way. If there is, try talking to a trusted family member or friend about it first.

Usually, when we feel like posting something negative it is because we are already feeling a bit rubbish ourselves. If you don't feel like you have someone to talk to about what's going on with you right now, you can always talk to us. Reach out to the Ditch the Label Community here, and we will listen to you no matter what.

6) How do you think it will make you feel afterwards?

So, it's actually a proven thing that the more we think negatively about other people, the more we beat ourselves up too. The chances are, you won't actually be feeling that great about yourself after you've commented or slid into someone's DMs with something mean. Reprogramming your thoughts into nice ones is a great way to stop your brain in its tracks, and will actually help you to think more positively about yourself.

Grab a pen and paper and write whatever the negative thing is that you want to send. Then underneath it, write a reason why you shouldn't, how it might make the other person feel, or something nice instead. Seeing this written out in front of you in your own handwriting might help you to see why it isn't the best idea. By writing something nice instead, you might be able to see how being kinder is easier and how it even makes you feel better.

7) Is it because they are famous/an influencer etc?

Just because someone is famous or has loads of followers, doesn't mean they won't care what is said about them. They are humans too with feelings and emotions, and families and lives that might be affected by what you say. It can be

super easy to forget that when they seem to only exist on Instagram or in tabloids, but they aren't immune to feeling bad.

8) How will it affect their lives?

There's a good chance that whatever you say will have an actual impact on someone's life. We know it might not seem like it when there is a screen and probably hundreds or maybe even thousands of miles between you, but whatever gets put out into the universe has the power to make waves and to damage someone's life, career or relationship beyond repair.

9) How would it affect you if you were on the receiving end?

OK so we know this is the kind of thing your teacher or your Mum used to say when they wanted to prove a point, but actually feeling empathy for other people is super important before you decide to say or send something negative online. If those notifications came popping up on your screen, the chances are you would feel a bit crap about the whole thing.

31 May 2019

Anonymous apps risk fuelling cyberbullying but they also fill a vital role

An article from **The Conversation.**

THE CONVERSATION

By Killian O'Leary, Lecturer in Consumer Behaviour, Lancaster University

When the anonymous social media app YOLO was launched in May 2019, it topped the iTunes downloads chart after just one week, despite the lack of a major marketing campaign. Designed to be used with social network Snapchat, YOLO lets users invite people to send them anonymous messages. Its viral popularity followed that of other apps, such as the now infamously defunct Yik Yak as well as Whisper, Secret, Spout, Swiflie and Sarahah. All these cater to a desire for anonymous interaction online.

The explosive popularity of YOLO has led to warnings of the same problem that led to Yik Yak's shutdown, namely that its anonymity could lead to cyberbullying and hate speech.

But in an age of online surveillance and self-censorship, proponents view anonymity as an essential component of privacy and free speech. And our own research on anonymous online interactions among teenagers in the UK and Ireland has revealed a wider range of interactions that extend beyond the toxic to the benign and even beneficial.

The problem with anonymous apps is the torrent of reports of cyberbullying, harassment and threats that appear to be even more of a feature than in regular social networks.

Psychologist John Suler, who specialises in online behaviour, describes this phenomenon as the 'online disinhibition effect'. This means people feel less accountable for their actions when they feel removed from their real identities.

The veil provided by anonymity enables people to become rude, critical, angry, hateful and threatening towards one another, without fear of repercussion. But this opportunity for uninhibited expression is also what makes anonymous apps both attractive to and beneficial for people who want to use them in a positive way.

Freedom from social media's tyranny

Recent studies highlight that young people are becoming increasingly dissatisfied with the narcissistic culture that dominates networks such as Facebook, Instagram and Snapchat.

Due to the nature of their design, these platforms encourage people to present idealised versions of themselves. Not only is this emotionally taxing, but deploying the camera filters and other image augmentation tools involved in these idealised presentations means this process can involve a significant workload.

Young people increasingly feel that social media can lead to anxiety and feelings of inadequacy that they take from constantly comparing themselves to unrealistic images of other people. In light of these pressures, it's less surprising that young people are increasingly turning to various forms of anonymous interaction that free them from the need to present a perfect avatar.

Instead, anonymous apps provide a forum for young people to engage in what they consider to be more authentic modes of interaction, expression and connection. This can take various forms. For some, anonymity opens up space to be honest about the problems they suffer and seek support for issues that carry stigma – such as anxiety, depression, self-harm, addiction and body dysphoria. It can provide an important outlet for catharsis and, at times, comfort.

For others, anonymity gives them a way to pronounce their harsh 'truths' on important social issues without fear of retribution for going against popular opinions of their peers.

One aspect of the idealised self-presentation of social media is supporting certain views because they are seen to be fashionable among a certain group of people, rather than because they are truly held beliefs.

This so-called 'virtue signalling' is part of the debate about the authenticity of interactions online. While anonymity doesn't necessarily create more intellectual discussion, it does provide a more open forum where people can represent their true opinions without fear of being ostracised or harassed for saying the wrong thing.

A ban would be shortsighted

Anonymity is not perfect, it is not always good, but equally it is not always bad.

Cyberbullying is undoubtedly a serious issue that needs to be tackled. Yet content moderation and the determination of what can, and cannot, be said or shared online is subjective. It is an imperfect system, but calls for an outright ban on anonymity may be short-sighted. They tend to underline the negative associations of anonymity without showing awareness of its positive potential.

What is truly needed is education. Certainly more needs to be done to educate young people about the perils of social media consumption. Updated curricula in schools, colleges and universities can, and should, do much more in this respect.

But equally, app designers and service providers need to become more aware of the negative effects that their offerings can have. Safeguarding should top the agendas of Silicon Valley companies, especially when they are targeting young people and freeing people to say whatever they like without fear of repercussions.

11 July 2019

Cyberbullying makes young people twice as likely to self harm or attempt suicide

By Sarah Knapton, Science Editor

Cyberbullying makes young people more than twice as likely to self-harm or attempt suicide, a major new study has shown.

The growth of social media has left many youngsters vulnerable to online bullying, which can include sending threatening, humiliating or intimidating messages or posting hurtful comments or images.

Around one third of young people claim to have been victims, but the new research suggests it can have damaging and deadly consequences.

Researchers at the Universities of Oxford, Swansea and Birmingham reviewed previous studies on cyberbullying which involved more than 150,000 under-25s across 30 countries over a 21-year period.

They found that cyberbullying raised the risk of self-harm or suicidal behaviour 2.3 times.

Professor Ann John, of Swansea University Medical School, who led the study, said:

'Prevention of cyberbullying should be included in school anti-bullying policies, alongside broader concepts such as digital citizenship, online peer support for victims, how an electronic bystander might appropriately intervene; and more specific interventions such as how to contact mobile phone companies and internet service providers to block, educate or identify users

'Suicide prevention and intervention is essential within any comprehensive anti-bullyingprogramme and should incorporate a whole-school approach to include awareness raising and training for staff and pupils.'

The researchers say that young people who are involved in cyberbullying should be screened for common mental disorders and self harm.

The study also found a strong link between being a cyber-victim and being a perpetrator.

This duality was found to particularly put males at higher risk of depression and suicidal behaviours.

Perpetrators were also around 20 per cent more likely to have self-harmed or attempted suicide than non-bullies.

The research also found that students who were cyber-victimised were less likely to report and seek help than those victimised by more traditional means.

22 April 2018

The research was published in the *Journal of Medical Internet Research.*

Online trolling and mental health: why there's nothing scarier than reality

Trolling online, like most things, probably started as a joke, a bit of fun which has slowly but surely escalated into the extremes. From the controversial, to the critical, to the horrendously offensive, trolls' comments online can spark arguments and damage targets' self-esteem, confidence and mental health: trolls entertaining themselves at the expense of others. Mental health is such a prevalent topic nowadays, yet when it comes to cyberbullying and online harassment from trolls, the conversation just doesn't seem to be there – even though the statistics are so shocking. So why aren't we talking about trolling more?

In the light of Halloween, we want to explore this topic more, because there's nothing scarier than the reality we're facing. What really goes on in the mind of online trolls; why do they torment and harass others? What can we do to prevent such behaviour? Read on to find out our thoughts.

We live in an age where we're living two lives: in reality and online. The rise of social media means that people have the freedom to post their whole lives online for everyone to see and judge. This increased accessibility and ability to connect with people the world over means that your life, thoughts and whole self are visible for the whole world to comment on, judge, criticise and make fun of.

This paves the way for internet trolls: bullies now have the opportunity to hide behind the security of online anonymity whilst throwing around mean comments and jokes, whether this be towards a celebrity, social group or individual. Trolling has been defined to encompass unsolicited and/or controversial comments intended to provoke, upset or argue with readers. A recent study found that online bullying has grown by 88% in just five years, with thousands of children and teenagers being targeted; however, no one is exempt from being the victim of trolling. Trolling predominantly manifests in people being made fun of and criticised for the sake of starting an argument to entertain themselves at the expense of others. I'm sure we've all seen examples of such behaviour, particularly in comments sections on social media. In some extreme situations, however, it has been reported that trolls have spread anti-Semitic messages, rape and death threats and encouragements to people to kill themselves.

There is obviously some deep-rooted problem within these people which needs addressing. Just why do they do it?

The largest reported reason surrounding why people troll is due to the anonymity of the internet: put simply, they can get away with it more so than real life. Research has also quoted 'temporary identity loss'; explaining that trolling may bring out the worst side in us, by lifting the moral constraints and social etiquette that regulate our behaviour in normal situations, fuelling abrasive reactions. Essentially, the internet and the online world is distant from reality so it seems like there are fewer consequences of online bullying compared with bullying in the physical world; this is obviously not the case.

Could it be that trolling is a status-enhancing activity: people looking to gain the greatest number of likes, laughs and shares to signal online popularity? This reminds me of Monica Lewinsky's TED talk that I watched recently in which she explains how we are in a culture of breaking each other down and profiting from others' embarrassment. I couldn't agree with her more. Bullies benefit from, and are entertained at, the expense of others. In this online society, the more outrageous the posts, the more clicks, likes and follows, and the more money which is generated. It's a disgusting and harmful cycle we must break from.

This desensitisation to the impact of such behaviours is not just facing individuals, but society as a whole. And this is where

the danger lies, because bullies don't consider the possibly disastrous impact their words and actions online can have on people's self-esteem, confidence and mental health.

Lewinsky herself discusses how, during the scandal with Bill Clinton, the comments regarding herself online drove her family to worry that she would take her own life. According to Mind, one in four people experience mental health problems every year, and a recent rise in hospital admissions of teenagers for suicidal thoughts and attempted suicides has been reportedly linked to an increase in cyberbullying. In order to tackle the issue of trolls, we need to look not only at the individuals, but work towards changing society's attitudes, values and inner-workings to truly generate change.

A quick Google search brings up hundreds of articles in which the advice 'Don't feed the trolls' is presented, encouraging that the best way to deal with trolls is ignore them – they thrive off the attention. But I think it's time we see this issue as it really is: abusive behaviour which can have devastating results. It's an issue which needs tackling. Whilst the internet is constantly expanding and evolving, faster than we can possibly monitor, we must take action. Taken to the extreme, trolling targets different ethnic, religious, racial groups. Some have encompassed such talk within hate speech, with Director of Public Prosecutions Alison Saunders at the Crown Prosecution Service commenting:

'Social media can be used to educate, entertain and enlighten, but there are also people who use it to bully, intimidate and harass. Ignorance is not a defence and

perceived anonymity is not an escape. Those who commit these acts, or encourage others to do the same, can and will be prosecuted.'

Is this a little extreme? Some may say that cracking down on trolls even through online reporting and blocking profiles and content is a threat to freedom of speech, but there's got to be a line drawn when your speech is created deliberately to make fun of others, be aggressive, critical, harmful and bully others without being provoked.

The phrase 'If you don't have anything nice to say, don't say it' comes to mind.

We are reminded every day of the real-life impact of online bullying. This is a topic we need to stop tiptoeing around. It is no longer any good or acceptable to pretend that this is not an issue, now is the time to take charge and take appropriate action. It's time we took responsibility for our and others' actions. Call it out when you see it. Report aggressive, offensive accounts. Don't just stand on the side-lines. It will make a difference.

31 October 2018

Vulnerable children are 'hounded' by cyberbullies in their bedrooms

By Natahsa Bernal

British children are being hounded by cyberbullies in their own bedrooms using smartphones which are fuelling an 'unprecedented' mental health crisis, the boss of the nation's largest children's charity has warned.

Barnardo's chief executive Javed Khan called on the Government, technology companies and schools to increase the help offered to young children and teenagers.

He backed calls for a legal duty of care on technology companies to keep children safe online. It follows guidance from the country's chief medical officer urging parents to ban smartphones from mealtimes and leave them outside of bedrooms at night in a move to curb social media addiction.

Mr Khan said: 'It used to be that any problem would remain at the school gates, and when you got home you are in a safe haven,' he said. 'Now at 3am that 'ping' sound will happen, and it might be the cyber bully, who has chased you into your bedroom.'

Mr Khan said that the UK is facing a growing children's mental health crisis that is part fueled by technology-related stress.

He cited rising levels of anxiety and stress among children aged between 13 and 15, many of whom are under the threshold for help through the NHS. Others, Mr Khan said, have to wait six months before they are given professional help.

'A whole generation of children are missing out on the support that they need,' he said.

'They are going to be a statistic in the NHS and the criminal justice system.'

He has welcomed the Government's implementation of an 'online safety' module in schools to teach children about the risks of technology and how to use it properly, which will be launched within the new sex education programme from next year.

However, he says that tech companies should be forced to be 'more transparent' with information relating to children on their sites.

'It's time for the Government to stand up and compel technology companies to do the right thing,' he commented.

'Tech needs to be designed with children's safety in mind and not as an afterthought. Tech companies and the Government needs to make sure that sites and tech need to be safe.'

Data published by Barnardo's last year showed that a quarter of children aged between 13 and 15 had communicated with a stranger on social media. This included 27% of girls and 33% of 14-year-olds.

'There are children who are switched on, who know how to remain safe. There are others that don't,' Mr Khan

commented. 'With the right controls in place, almost all tech is a good thing for schools and children.'

Mr Khan welcomed calls from health secretary Matt Hancock to remove addictive content online and to hold social media companies to account but says 'words must be followed by urgent action'.

'Children can't afford to wait another two years for a change in the law. Any delay to act could put another generation in danger,' he said.

A recent YouGov poll found that almost half of UK children were worried about returning to class after the school holidays because of bullying. Experts warned that despite laws and procedures being introduced to stamp out bullying in classrooms, it has become 'normalised' and remains a major issue.

Of the 1,003 secondary-age students surveyed, 39% said bullying had affected their grades, 38% said they had missed school because they were so frightened of bullies. More than a fifth (22%) said bullying had become so intense that they had been forced to change schools.

7 February 2019

This woman's son took his own life after he was bullied on social media – every parent should listen to her message

Lucy Alexander has shared the tragic story of her son, Felix, who was hit by a train after repeatedly being told he was worthless, ugly, and hated by everybody.

By Stephanie Balloo

A mum has made an emotional plea for parents to learn how to use social media after her son, who had been cyberbullied, took his own life.

Seventeen-year-old Felix Alexander had repeatedly been told he was worthless, ugly and hated by anonymous bullies online – he tragically died after being hit by a train.

Now his mother Lucy Alexander has teamed up with police to share the heartbreaking story in a bid to warn parents to become familiar with social media, talk to their children about how they use it, and report any problems.

Lucy appears in a video to talk about how 'kind and caring Felix' had a bright future, but that the problems began after he became isolated and excluded at school. They became worse when he moved to a new school, and started spending time on social media.

The *Birmingham Mail* reports how she said Felix had been the victim of a string of negative comments on a site which allowed users to post anonymous comments or ask questions without revealing who they are.

Despite not having his own computer, Lucy explained that when he heard about the cruel comments her son had even searched them out.

At the age of 14, Felix was receiving negative comments on social media sites 'every day'.

She says: 'It was from people he knew, people he didn't know. He was called black rat, ugly, that he was worthless and that everybody hated him. Just general nastiness.

'They didn't understand or think through the consequences of what they said and did.

'Every day he had something from someone.'

Lucy goes on to explain the horrifying morning of 27 April, 2016 when the school had called to inform the family Felix hadn't made it into school.

She tells how she – along with her husband – had chased a police car after her gut feeling told her "something horrible had happened".

In the video – posted by West Mercia Police – Lucy urges parents to communicate with their children and ensure they utilise the support available from social media platforms.

She adds: 'From the moment you give your child a phone, you need to have a conversation going with them all the time, what they're doing who they're doing it with, what platforms they're using.'

Parents should always report cyberbullying, evidence it, take screenshots and talk to the local police, she advised.

She said: 'This is something that never occurred to me when Felix was young, I didn't realise anybody could help or advise me.'

The video comes almost exactly one year after Lucy published a heartbreaking letter urging children to 'always be kind", which hit the headlines across the country.

The letter read: 'I am appealing to children to be kind ALWAYS and never stand by and leave bullying unreported.

'Be that one person prepared to stand up to unkindness. You will never regret being a good friend.'

12 October 2017

UK to introduce world-first online safety laws

The Government have unveiled tough new measures to ensure the UK is the safest place in the world to be online.

◆ **Independent regulator will be appointed to enforce stringent new standards**

◆ **Social media firms must abide by mandatory 'duty of care' to protect users and could face heavy fines if they fail to deliver**

◆ **Measures are the first of their kind in the world in the fight to make the internet a safer place**

In the first online safety laws of their kind, social media companies and tech firms will be legally required to protect their users and face tough penalties if they do not comply.

As part of the Online Harms White Paper, a joint proposal from the Department for Digital, Culture, Media & Sport and the Home Office, a new independent regulator will be introduced to ensure companies meet their responsibilities.

This will include a mandatory 'duty of care', which will require companies to take reasonable steps to keep their users safe and tackle illegal and harmful activity on their services. The regulator will have effective enforcement tools, and we are consulting on powers to issue substantial fines, block access to sites and potentially to impose liability on individual members of senior management.

Prime Minister Theresa May said:

'The internet can be brilliant at connecting people across the world – but for too long these companies have not done enough to protect users, especially children and young people, from harmful content.

That is not good enough, and it is time to do things differently. We have listened to campaigners and parents, and are putting a legal duty of care on internet companies to keep people safe.

Online companies must start taking responsibility for their platforms, and help restore public trust in this technology.'

A range of harms will be tackled as part of the Online Harms White Paper, including inciting violence and violent content, encouraging suicide, disinformation, cyberbullying and children accessing inappropriate material.

There will be stringent requirements for companies to take even tougher action to ensure they tackle terrorist and child sexual exploitation and abuse content.

The new proposed laws will apply to any company that allows users to share or discover user-generated content or interact with each other online. This means a wide range of companies of all sizes are in scope, including social media platforms, file-hosting sites, public discussion forums, messaging services, and search engines.

A regulator will be appointed to enforce the new framework. The Government is now consulting on whether the regulator should be a new or existing body. The regulator will be funded by industry in the medium term, and the Government is exploring options such as an industry levy to put it on a sustainable footing.

A 12-week consultation on the proposals has also been launched today. Once this concludes we will then set out

the action we will take in developing our final proposals for legislation.

Tough new measures set out in the White Paper include:

◆ A new statutory 'duty of care' to make companies take more responsibility for the safety of their users and tackle harm caused by content or activity on their services.

◆ Further stringent requirements on tech companies to ensure child abuse and terrorist content is not disseminated online.

◆ Giving a regulator the power to force social media platforms and others to publish annual transparency reports on the amount of harmful content on their platforms and what they are doing to address this.

◆ Making companies respond to users' complaints, and act to address them quickly.

◆ Codes of practice, issued by the regulator, which could include measures such as requirements to minimise the spread of misleading and harmful disinformation with dedicated fact checkers, particularly during election periods.

◆ A new 'Safety by Design' framework to help companies incorporate online safety features in new apps and platforms from the start.

◆ A media literacy strategy to equip people with the knowledge to recognise and deal with a range of deceptive and malicious behaviours online, including catfishing, grooming and extremism.

The UK remains committed to a free, open and secure Internet. The regulator will have a legal duty to pay due regard to innovation, and to protect users' rights online, being particularly mindful to not infringe privacy and freedom of expression.

Recognising that the Internet can be a tremendous force for good, and that technology will be an integral part of any solution, the new plans have been designed to promote a culture of continuous improvement among companies. The new regime will ensure that online firms are incentivised to develop and share new technological solutions, like Google's 'Family Link' and Apple's Screen Time app, rather than just complying with minimum requirements. Government has balanced the clear need for tough regulation with its ambition for the UK to be the best place in the world to start and grow a digital business, and the new regulatory framework will provide strong protection for our citizens while driving innovation by not placing an impossible burden on smaller companies.

8 April 2019

UK universities urged to do more to tackle online harassment

As new guidance is issued, expert says less than a quarter have adequate procedures.

By David Batty

Universities UK has published guidance for its members on how to tackle online harassment including cyberstalking, trolling and sexting.

Internet safety experts say less than a quarter of UK universities have adequate procedures to deal with harmful or illegal online behaviour by students and staff, including the possession and sharing of child abuse images.

UUK, which represents higher education institutions, has recommended that universities clearly set out how they expect students and staff to behave online, such as in chat groups, and that they make reference to online harassment in disciplinary policies and procedures and their student code of conduct.

Prof. Emma Bond, whose work on the issue at the University of Suffolk was highlighted as a model of good practice in the UUK guidance, said online harassment had reached a watershed moment with the first generation of students who grew up with smartphones entering higher education.

She said many universities failed to recognise the severity of the problem, particularly the issue of students possessing or sharing sexual images of under-18s, including selfies and photos or videos of their school peers, which could be classified as child abuse images.

'What students are not thinking about as they come to university and are now 18 or 19 is the legality of still having images of younger school peers in their cloud storage or on their devices,' Bond said.

'University policy and staff have not kept kept abreast of it at all. Very few – less than a quarter at most – have adequate procedures to deal with online harassment. It's really ad

hoc as to whether or not universities even record these incidents. Some have got policies, some haven't. There's no uniformity at all.'

In May, a *Guardian* investigation revealed that hundreds of university students had been disciplined or expelled for making sexually explicit, homophobic or racist comments on social media.

The UUK guidance calls for a zero-tolerance approach to online harassment and for vice-chancellors and other senior managers to be held accountable for online safety. It recommends that staff receive specialist training from internet safety experts or the police, and that universities work with and better support victims of online harassment.

Prof. Debra Humphris, the chair of Universities UK's student policy network and vice-chancellor of the University of Brighton, said: 'Misuse of social media and other online platforms can leave students exposed to abuse, affecting their mental health and wellbeing, disrupting their education and potentially impacting on their future employability and career prospects.

'In order to tackle online harassment and cyberbullying, we must consider the specific threats it poses as part of our duty of care to all students. This needs to be acknowledged across institutions as part of strategic work to tackle violence, harassment and hate crime.'

Bond said Suffolk's digital civility project had advised students on how they could get help from the Internet Watch Foundation (IWF), which acts as a de facto watchdog for online child abuse in the UK, to safely remove potentially illegal content from their devices and storage and how to report the non-consensual sharing of sexual images of adults to the Revenge Porn Helpline. 'We made sure all our staff had training on how to handle a disclosure of online sexual abuse,' she said.

An IWF spokeswoman said that over the past two years the charity had increasingly been approached by UK universities seeking to improve online safety for staff and students.

'They're concerned about preventing either the accidental or deliberate finding of child sexual abuse material on the internet, and consider that to be a crucial element of their cybersecurity and student welfare.'

The spokeswoman said the IWF was working with five UK universities – Sheffield Hallam, Nottingham Trent, Manchester Metropolitan, Surrey and Hertfordshire – to address this issue.

One of the women targeted by male Warwick University students in a Facebook 'rape chat' group welcomed the UUK recommendations. Danielle, not her real name, said that in her case staff failed to understand the consequences of violent and sexual threats online.

'There was this attitude that you can't be a victim because nothing happened to you in real life. There needs to be better training to ensure staff don't have those misconceptions,' she said.

A Department for Education spokesperson said: 'Online harassment is unacceptable in any circumstance and can have a devastating impact on the victims. We expect universities to follow this guidance and put robust policies and procedures in place, including effective disciplinary processes and ensure that victims are supported.'

2 September 2019

Entrepreneur's anti-bullying app helps half a million kids

Michael Brennan co-founded Tootoot after he experienced bullying at school – now he is taking on bullying within sports clubs and the workplace.

By Jonathan Symcox

An entrepreneur who endured years of bullying has used his experience to help half a million children and young people.

Michael Brennan, now 28, suffered at the hands of bullies for years at primary and secondary schools in Essex and it continued even when his family moved to the North East.

'It started off with verbal and physical abuse,' the entrepreneur told *BusinessCloud*.

'When I moved to a secondary school in Berwick-upon-Tweed, in Northumberland, that's where the online problems were caused.

'It was at the start of the explosion of social media, when platforms like Facebook were becoming popular.'

Anti-bullying helplines eased his problems but didn't fix them, as they couldn't feed the information back to schools – a problem he has now fixed through Tootoot.

The platform allows students in schools, colleges and universities to anonymously report incidents of bullying and cyberbullying and make it easier for schools to manage and deal with. It also helps them to speak up about issues including mental health and racism.

'If schools and parents are looking at ways to prevent bullying and cyber bullying, it's important that young people are encouraged to speak up – and in particular have safe avenues to report,' said CEO Brennan, who founded the business with CTO Kieran Innes in 2015.

'We need to use and embrace technology because that's what young people are using and where the issues such as cyberbullying are coming from.'

A thousand schools have used Tootoot's various anti-bullying programmes, while 500 are currently using its software. Brennan says 280,000 children and young people are currently active and registered on the software.

In June last year the firm, which has raised around £1 million in funding to date, moved its headquarters from Berwick-upon-Tweed to the MSP tech incubator in Manchester, although it retains sales bases in the North East and Scotland. It made sense to move HQ, says Brennan, because there are 3,000 schools in the North West and that is where its investment is based.

Former Great Britain rugby league player Terry Flanagan is its chairman while Tangerine PR and The Juice Academy founder Sandy Lindsay and AO.com non-executive director Chris Hopkinson are among the investors.

Huddersfield Town is one of two Premier League clubs already using a sports version of the app, along with lower-division clubs Rochdale and Blackpool and organisations in other sports.

'As long as people are interacting together, there will be challenges of culture; of boundaries for bullying and banter; and the more serious concerns of reporting safeguarding issues such as child abuse, radicalisation and extremism,' Brennan continued.

'The problem isn't going to go away. When we introduce our platforms and apps to a school or a sports club, we explain that they are setting themselves up for the future, the next five to ten years, as opposed to putting a quick fix in for six months and saying 'we've changed the culture'.

'Ultimately it's going to take a number of years, in sport in particular, to change that culture from the awful problems that have been occurring inside some clubs.'

The firm has seen 45,000 concerns reported across education and sport in the last 24 months, despite the latter app only being live for the last ten. One in ten young people registered on the app have used it for that purpose.

Brennan is looking to raise between a further £750,000 and £1 million in the next three months to further develop Tootoot's app for the workplace. As well as speaking to current shareholders, he is targeting larger backers, such as private equity houses and angel investors, to support international growth.

'We've secured our first nine pilot customers for 'workplace' – two of them are enterprise organisations with 5,000 employees or more,' said Brennan. 'The other seven are smaller, with 250 employees. It's been a great start.

'If you think of the sexual harassment problems in some of the larger organisations that have recently been highlighted, a lot of it comes from individuals not feeling confident or having a way to speak up or around the people causing the problems.

'I do see these problems becoming worse. We have to ensure people have the avenues to speak up.'

28 January 2019

Cyberbullying: four steps to protect your kids

An article from **The Conversation.**

By Ryan Broll, Assistant Professor, University of Guelph

THE CONVERSATION

In a typical classroom of 25 to 30 students, eight to ten children – a third of the class – have been cyberbullied at some point in their lifetime. About three or four students are likely to have bullied others online.

High-profile cases like those involving Amanda Todd and Rehtaeh Parsons, both of whom committed suicide after being bullied online, demonstrate how harmful this can be.

Research consistently finds that cyberbullying is associated with a number of social, emotional and academic problems. Young people who are involved in cyberbullying, either as offender or victim, are also more likely to think about and attempt suicide.

Compared to other forms of bullying, the 'always on' and viral nature of cyberbullying may exacerbate these problems and a recent Canadian study suggests that the harmful impact of cyberbullying can persist into adulthood.

The days of viewing bullying as 'kids being kids' are long gone. As former US President Barack Obama declared at the White House Conference on Bullying Prevention in 2011: 'If there's one goal of this conference, it's to dispel the myth that bullying is just a harmless rite of passage or an inevitable part of growing up. It's not. Bullying can have destructive consequences for our young people.'

Annual events, like International Stand Up to Bullying Day on 23 February 2018, and Pink Shirt Day on 28 February 2018, help draw attention to cyberbullying and encourage action. But preventing cyberbullying is also a daily task that requires many people to work together.

As a researcher who studies cyberbullying, I have found that among parents, teachers and the police, parents have the most important role to play in prevention. Naturally, parents want to protect their children, and may wonder what they can do to prevent cyberbullying.

Fortunately, research suggests some practical steps that parents can take to reduce their child's risk:

1. Accept your child's online life

Many adults clearly distinguish between their online and offline lives, but young people rarely make such distinctions – their offline and online lives are one and the same.

As Danah Boyd explains in her book *It's Complicated: The Social Lives of Networked Teens*, young people increasingly socialise online because today's parents restrict their ability to socialise offline much more than in the past. Teens still want to spend time with their friends, but because they are often not allowed to hang out at the mall or the movies, their socialising has moved online.

Given the importance of technology to teens, well-meaning suggestions like 'Nobody cares what you had for breakfast"' or 'Just delete your account' are likely to be met with an exaggerated eye roll.

If a child has been cyberbullied, taking away their access to technology – even as a well-intentioned safety precaution – may further victimize them and reduce their likelihood of telling adults about future incidents.

2. Set rules for online interaction

Accepting technology does not mean ignoring it. About one in eight parents do not set any rules about what their children do online.

Yet setting rules about when children can go online, and what they can and cannot do, is one of the simplest and most effective ways of preventing cyberbullying, according to research.

Children are also less likely to cyberbully others when they believe that their parents are likely to punish them for such behaviour.

The American Academy of Pediatrics specifically recommends setting limits on screen time for young people.

While their recommendations deal with a range of issues, other research indicates that young people's risk of cyberbullying increases as they spend more time online.

3. Teach respect and responsibility online

Parents should teach their children how to behave online, just as they teach them how to use manners and be respectful offline. On the internet, this is known as 'netiquette,' and it reduces young people's involvement in cyberbullying.

Behaving responsibly online is a skill that needs to be taught. A popular analogy compares society's approaches to introducing young people to two powerful machines: Vehicles and the internet.

Before teenagers are allowed to drive, they have to follow a series of graduated steps that includes a great deal of learning and practice under close supervision. And yet, when children begin using technology, we often tell them to 'be smart' and hope for the best.

Admittedly, it can be difficult for many parents to keep up with trends in technology – popular apps and social networking sites come and go quickly. Rather than being seen as an obstacle, parents can embrace these innovations as an opportunity for their children to teach them about their favourite apps and websites.

This allows parents to learn what their children are doing, while offering a non-threatening opportunity to ensure that their children know all of their Instagram followers or Snapchat friends and that they are not publicly sharing personal details.

4. Monitor online activities

It is important that parents monitor their children's online activities just like they monitor their offline activities.

Parents are accustomed to asking their children where they are going, who they will be with, and what time they will be home. Fewer ask these types of questions online: What websites are you visiting? Who are you talking to? What are you doing online?

Research has found that this type of parental mediation greatly reduces children's likelihood of being cyberbullied. Making use of built-in parental controls and safety features may be also be helpful.

As technology becomes more portable, best practices like keeping computers in high-traffic areas of the home become more difficult. As a result, active parental monitoring is becoming increasingly important.

Parents' efforts should be tailored to their child's age and maturity. And, despite a parent's best intentions, their child may still experience cyberbullying.

If this happens, parents should listen to their children, take their concerns seriously and seek help from others when necessary.

20 February 2018

Workers need to be protected from cyberbullying. Here's how   THE CONVERSATION

An article published in collaboration with The Conversation.

By Natalie D'Souza, Lecturer, School of Management, Massey University

Nurses are a target for bullies more often than any other healthcare workers, and the bullying can take many forms.

My research shows that nurses are particularly vulnerable to cyberbullying by patients and their relatives, which can cross the boundary between the workplace and home. This highlights the need for employers to take cyberbullying seriously and to take active steps to protect employees from it.

Cyberbullying can be especially damaging

Cyberbullying is a growing problem both in New Zealand and internationally. It can take place in any workplace, but researchers have identified clear hotspots such as hospitals, schools and customer services.

Reporting of workplace cyberbullying varies dramatically because there is no consensus on how to define it. Generally, cyberbullying is more complex and insidious than traditional forms of workplace bullying.

It can be described as unwanted or aggressive behaviour(s), perpetrated through electronic media, that may harm, threaten or demoralise the recipient(s), and can occur beyond work time. Because workplace cyberbullying crosses the barrier between work and home, it can leave people feeling trapped and unable to cope.

Cyberbullying can take several forms, including harassment, cyberstalking, denigration and exclusion.

No escape

It is easy to imagine the threat people feel when they receive anonymous and unwanted texts, or the ongoing humiliation resulting from being abused on social media. In my study, nurses described the distress of not only having false allegations made about them on a public platform, but also of the potential repercussions on their reputation and career. One case of anonymous cyberbullying proved particularly difficult as there was little the organisation could do to intervene, with the abuse spanning several years.

Public forms of cyberbullying are also likely to have a much broader scope of harm – not only for the targets but also for the organisations involved. Customer or patient complaints on public forums may harm the target's career as well as affecting the organisation's reputation.

Likewise, the constant access provided by electronic devices is also likely to make targets of cyberbullying feel trapped. They have little chance of escaping the bullying at home or replenishing their coping resources.

Cyberbullying easily circumvents common safety measures used to protect nurses, such as security offers or trespass notices. It introduces a new vulnerability for nurses and employees in public roles.

Nurses have a responsibility to care for patients, which can make it difficult for them to block communication with relatives, even when they are being bullied, directly or via electronic channels. In one example, a patient's mother would call to ask for help for her son, but then start abusing the nurse, who could not block the calls in case it was a genuine emergency.

How to approach prevention

Over time, cyberbullying can have a severe impact on the health of victims. They can reach a point where they feel forced to leave their place of work.

Organisations have an ethical and legal responsibility to ensure the health and safety of employees. There are also substantial financial costs associated with not preventing

workplace cyberbullying. Australia's Productivity Commission estimated the cost at A$6 billion to A$36 billion per year.

Many organisations aren't well equipped to deal with workplace cyberbullying. Few have a relevant policy in place. This can often unintentionally signal to employees that cyberbullying is an issue they have to deal with on their own.

There are several actions that organisations and industry need to take. They should clearly communicate what cyberbullying might look like within the workplace. They should adopt a clear policy, along with reporting channels and processes, to indicate to employees that the organisation takes cyberbullying seriously.

Any policies should include cyberbullying from sources outside the organisation, including customers, clients, students and patients. Finally, organisations must be prepared to take all reports and complaints of cyberbullying seriously, and support employees through this process.

At a much broader level, industry and professional bodies can address workplace cyberbullying in their current policies, codes of conduct and training resources. An industry-based approach to prevention and intervention is much more likely to be effective in addressing profession-specific risk factors such as those faced by health-care workers.

At a national level, it is crucial that workplace cyberbullying – and traditional bullying, for that matter – are recognised in law as risks to employee health and safety.

12 February 2018

MACRO

'Mateship' of small, closed communities

Inadequate (national + industry) policy and support

Bullying culture

Work-related pressures

MESO

No suitable individual to report to/intervene

Inadequate policy and mgmt.

Institutional bullying

Target perceptions of self-mgmt.

MICRO

Perpetrator-related features (culture)

Cyberbullies are also victims – they need help too

An article from The Conversation.

By Ann John, Clinical Professor of Public Health and Psychiatry, Swansea University

THE CONVERSATION

Cyberbullying is very different to traditional bullying. Relationships between victims and perpetrators do not need to be physically close, they don't need to be in the same class or even in the same school, for example. It can easily be anonymous, which may lower inhibitions to behave in a mean or hurtful way. It doesn't stop once someone is at home, and isn't limited by time of day or night. And the potential exposure and embarrassment of the victim is on a much larger scale.

There may be no respite or sanctuary for a victim of cyberbullying. Messages can be sent and received via mobiles in secret or through anonymous apps, with no one to step in and stop it.

Being bullied is associated with self-harm and suicidal behaviours, as well as mental health problems such as anxiety and depression. But what about cyberbullying? The stakes are high with greater exposure to peers and it can be persistent, so it's possible the impact could be more serious, too?

For our latest research, we systematically gathered all the studies on cyberbullying since the mid-1990s, to explore the association between it and self-harm and suicidal behaviours. We looked at information from more than 150,000 children and young people, from 30 different countries.

We found that approximately 13 in every 100 children and young people aged under 25 have experienced cyberbullying. And those who become victims of cyberbullying are more than twice as likely to self-harm and enact suicidal behaviours. Interestingly, perpetrators of cyberbullying are also more likely to experience suicidal thoughts and behaviours, although to a lesser extent.

We also found a link between being a cybervictim and a cyberbully, with at least one in 20 young people involved in both. It seems that all young people involved in cyberbullying, whether as victims or bullies, are vulnerable to self-harm and suicidal behaviours. This duality was found to put male cyberbullies and/or victims, in particular, at higher risk of depression and suicidal behaviours.

Ending the cycle

Evidently, we need new, more effective ways to try to stop cyberbullying once and for all. There are many impressive initiatives trying to deal with this type of bullying. But it is becoming increasingly difficult for adults to keep up with this rapidly changing environment, so we really need to look to young people for help stopping it. Our findings also make clear that anti-bullying programmes and protocols should address the needs of both victims and perpetrators in a more balanced way. We found that students who were cyber-victimised were less likely to report the bullying and seek help than those victimised in more traditional ways. So school and college staff need to do more to encourage them to seek help, as well as be trained to recognise the signs.

This behaviour should also be seen as an opportunity to support vulnerable young cyberbullies, rather than simply discipline them. These associated risks cannot be ignored, and punishment does not help young people address them. School exclusion or time away from the classroom (a common response from teachers to deal with cyberbullying) might contribute to an individual's sense of isolation and lead to feelings of hopelessness – also often associated with suicidal behaviours in adolescents.

There is no doubt that cyberbullying needs to be considered by policy makers who deliver bullying prevention and safe internet use programmes, too. While schools do run awareness activities, national bodies should also start providing online support and advice for victims and perpetrators. It's important that young people are told how to intervene as a bystander as well.

Families and communities can also do more. Though it can be hard for adults to keep up with the latest platforms or online celebrities, it is important to discuss online activity with young people from an early age. Just as in real-life social situations, children need to learn how to behave on the internet. It can be as simple as talking about how to behave online, how seemingly funny comments can impact on another person, and issues of consent when sharing videos and information.

Dealing with any form of bullying is not easy, but it can make all the difference to an isolated person. It can be difficult to have sympathy for a bully, but if we can all keep in mind that victims and bullies are sometimes one and the same – they are all vulnerable children and young people – we can start to give them the support they really need.

5 February 2018

How to report bullying or abuse on social media

Social Media businesses are governed by the laws of the country in which they are head-quartered, but they are also expected to comply with local laws where they operate. Most Social Media sites have a reporting system in place aimed at flagging inappropriate content; however, they do come under a lot of criticism for not taking online safety seriously enough.

Facebook

They do not tolerate bullying or abuse and say that once they are aware of it, they will remove bullying content and may disable the account of anyone who is bullying another. They adhere to a set of Community Standards, which include what Facebook will not tolerate:

◆ Pages that identify and shame private individuals

◆ Images that have been altered to degrade private individuals

◆ Photos or videos of physical bullying posted to shame the victim

◆ Sharing personal information to blackmail or harass people

◆ Repeatedly targeting other people with unwanted friend requests or messages.

Using the Report Links which appear on the page, you can report bullying to Facebook. A 'drop-down arrow' should appear giving you a menu option to report the image, post or comment.

You can unfriend or block a person from Facebook. Click on their profile, on the message dropdown you will see the option to 'unfriend' and/or 'block'.

Twitter

If a person sends you a tweet or replies to a tweet with a comment that you don't like, you can unfollow that person. To stop them from further contacting you, you can block them. If you receive unwanted replies or abuse or threats from someone on Twitter, you can report them direct to Twitter https://support.twitter.com/forms/abusiveuser

You can protect your tweets so that people can only follow you if you approve them first. Do this by going into the 'settings' menu, then 'security and privacy' and ticking the 'protect my tweets' box.

To remove or block someone on Twitter, click on the button with a head icon on it next to the 'Follow' button on a user's profile. When you click on this you will see a menu with the options to 'block' the user to prevent them from seeing your profile and you can also 'report for spam', which will alert Twitter to any users who are abusing the service.

YouTube

If you feel a video you have seen on YouTube is inappropriate, you can 'flag' this by clicking on the little flag at the bottom right of the video. YouTube will then look at it to see if it breaks their terms of use. If it does, they will remove it.

YouTube state that videos with hate content, graphic violence or nudity cannot be uploaded so if you see one, report it as inappropriate.

To remove someone from your YouTube page, go to your account page and click on 'all contacts' in the 'Friends and Contacts' section. Choose which person you wish to unfriend and click on 'remove contact'. Once you have done this, the person will no longer be on your 'share video' list.

If you receive abusive, bullying or threatening comments on YouTube, you can report them and they will investigate https://www.youtube.com/reportabuse.

Instagram

Bullying or abuse on Instagram can take place in a number of ways:

◆ Negative Comments

◆ Fake Profiles

◆ Hacking Accounts

Instagram's advice is to block and unfollow the person who is being abusive. To block someone on Instagram, tap their username to open their profile, tap the three dots and press the option to 'block user'.

Snapchat

Bullying through Snapchat takes place in a number of different ways, including:

◆ Taking Screenshots of images without permission

◆ Sending pictures without permission

◆ Negative comments

If this happens to you, you can block a 'friend':

◆ Tap the Menu icon

◆ Select 'My Friends'

◆ Locate their name in the list and swipe right across their name

◆ To delete them, press Delete

To block someone who added you on Snapchat:

◆ Tap 'added me' on the Profile Screen

- Tap their name and tap the 'Wheel Icon' next to their name
- Press 'block'

This will prevent them from sending you Snaps or Chats or from viewing your content.

If a person is bullying or harassing you or you receive an inappropriate image, report it by completing their online form https://support.snapchat.com/en-US/i-need-help.

WhatsApp

Legally, you have to be over 16 to use WhatsApp. As this is a messaging service, bullying can happen in many ways via WhatsApp. Once you install the App, it checks your address book and connects you automatically to anyone else you know who is using the App. You can block and delete a contact who may be bullying you through WhatsApp:

- Click on their name
- Using the drop-down menu, choose to 'block' the person.

You can find out more by emailing WhatsApp at support@whatsapp.com.

Some safety information

- Keep it Private – don't post anything on a social networking site that identifies your real name, address, phone number, school etc. as this will enable a stranger to contact you in real life. Be careful you don't identify your friends too.
- Never upload anything that might embarrass you at a later date. Things you post on the Internet stay there and can come back and cause problems for you later on; for instance, when you go for an interview for college or university or apply for a job. If you're happy for the world to see the photo or comment, hit send. If you're not, don't upload it!!! Once you've hit send, you have lost control of that image or comment forever.
- With today's technology, many of us have a camera available at all times. Never feel pressurised into taking pictures of yourself that you wouldn't want others to see. Always trust your gut instinct over this. As before, once you hit send, you have lost control over that image and this can cause immense anxiety and stress.
- If you ever use a shared computer, whether it be at home, at school, a library or Internet café, never forget to log off once you have finished your session or when you close the browser. If you don't, the next user may be able to access the sites you have been using under your name.
- Many sites enable you to 'check in' or post your location each time you post a status update. Whilst this can let your friends know where you are, places you're visiting and things you might be doing, it can also mean that people you don't know can also view this information – especially if your profile is public. Go into the 'Settings' menu of the social networking site or app, scroll to the 'Security and Privacy' section and turn off or uncheck the 'location' box.

Keep yourself safe

- If someone makes you feel uncomfortable, embarrassed or afraid online, you need to tell someone immediately. If someone suggests meeting up with you in real life, again, tell someone immediately. This is a huge concern, especially if they have suggested you keep it a secret. No matter how much a person tells you about themselves, if you don't know them really well in the 'real world, they are still a stranger and may not be telling you the truth.

- There have been a number of cases of adults pretending to be young people online and trying to engage other young people in inappropriate activities. This is called 'Grooming' and is a criminal offence. The Child Exploitation and Online Protection Centre (CEOP) investigate cases of grooming on the Internet and sex abuse and incidents can be reported by clicking the red button on the top right-hand corner of their website https://www.ceop.police.uk/safety-centre/.

- Don't get into an argument or post offensive, bullying or abusive material online. Never post anything which promotes physical harm or make threats to anyone. Don't spread rumours or make up false information about a person and don't encourage others to harass someone. It is defamatory if you say untrue things about a person which can give them a bad reputation and it can also be seen as harassment – which is a criminal offence in the UK.

- You are not allowed to upload a picture or video of anyone without their permission. Never set up a social networking site in someone else's name or upload false information about them.

Of course, all sites have a responsibility to keep their users safe and to ensure that all reports of cyberbullying and abuse are dealt with effectively; however, we, as users of such sites, also have a responsibility to make sure we are using them in a safe, respectful and appropriate manner.

January 2018

Professional sports, cyberbullies and why enough is enough

Blogpost by Sally Mahers

Bullying, in it's traditional form, has been going on since the beginning of time. That was when your bully had to face you. To say what he or she thought to your face in front of an audience and back up his attacks. Probably to physically assault you too.

These days bullies can do their bullying from the comfort of their bedroom, lounge or office desk. They can do their bullying without ever having to face their victim or show their face. They can literally be nameless and faceless and they can say whatever they like. They can say things they would almost definitely never say to your face too.

Sadly cyberbullying is on the rise and over 34% of students acknowledge that they have experienced cyberbullying (cyberbullying.org). This said, all schools and most youth organisations have a cyberbullying policy with clear guidelines and consequences.

The same, sadly, cannot be said in professional sports. The online abuse levelled at professional sports stars, staff, coaches and referees is on the rise.

How bad is it?

According to Kick It Out's study, there have been an estimated 134,400 discriminatory posts this season related to the Premier League alone.

That equates to:

- 16,800 discriminatory posts a month
- 551 of them per day
- One abusive mention every 2.6 minutes

Strangely, when sports stars get abused on social media, they are often advised to turn the other cheek. Let's just break that down for a minute.

Turn the other cheek. That's it. That's often the advice. Scroll on. Ignore it. Move on.

Whilst that is sound enough advice (Do not feed the trolls) it does beg the question – Why should they?

If the comments levelled at sports stars and pros were made to young adults and children there WOULD be consequences. So why are there not any consequences if people make these comments to adults? Do comments not affect adults? Because you're an adult you should be able to deal with them? To ignore them?

But sports stars should just 'turn the other cheek'. The main problem is there is no line. No consequence for their actions. If there is no line the level you can go to in terms of abuse will just go up and up.

'It's freedom of speech,' say many. It's not about freedom of speech though. It's about common decency. And if there is no barometer for what that should look like then it will only increase and keep increasing. It has to be stamped out.

Policing online trolling and bullying is VERY difficult. There are just so many messages, so many people, so many faceless accounts. What that doesn't mean, however, is that sports pros and clubs should just turn the other cheek.

The funny thing about all this is that is always a 'social media policy' for players and staff. Guidelines players and staff have to follow and to adhere to. Yet there is NO policy for supporters of the sport. That HAS to change.

Cyberbullies need to be tackled and addressed head on. Earlier this week, inspired by a tweet levelled at one of their players injured during a game, Elite League hockey club Coventry Blaze released their own statement regarding social media:

Whilst it still remains tough to police and regulate 'questionable' posts the Blaze have, at least, made their feelings on the matter very clear.

'As an organisation we will not tolerate social media communications which are clearly inappropriate and offensive towards any member of the club or which go beyond the realms of an acceptable nature. Personal insults or comments that show little regard for the wellbeing of any member of the club are simply not acceptable.

It's often easy to post an opinion on social media channels without a second thought given to any possible consequences or the well being of the person to whom it may be directed.

We would encourage all supporters to please consider that any post on any platform becomes *a public record, whether intended as something light-hearted or not, posts which might appear harmless to you, could be construed as offensive by others, or have a severe impact on the well-being of others.*

The Blaze reserve the right to, have, and will, deny entrance to our games to any individual who does not show consideration of the above.'

The Blaze have publicly come out in support of their staff including denying entrance to their home games. This is a great example of a sports club CLEARLY stating where the line is. It is never going to address every online troll but it is certainly a step in the right direction and something all sports clubs and leagues should be doing.

It is time for sports organisations to stand up in support of their staff and players. It is time for their to be a clear line in the sand and it is time for social media platforms to get better at policing online bullying.

As individuals all we can do is shout louder than the trolls. To make more noise than them, to report them and keep pushing for basic respect and decency towards professional sports men and women.

9 October 2018

The above information is reprinted with kind permission from Sally Mahers.
© 2019 Mahers Consulting

www.mahersconsulting.co.uk

How to deal with internet trolls

With a lot of our daily interactions happening online, it is easy to feel safe and confident on the internet. It's important that your children feel confident and happy online, but aware of what they can do and how you can help them if things aren't so positive.

What is an internet troll?

An internet troll is someone who constantly harasses a person on the internet through unwanted comments, page posts, messages, response videos and replies. These responses are usually made to upset, taunt, anger or bully, in other cases, gain attention, blackmail or control.

Why do they do it?

Psychologists believe that people are less inhibited by what they say online due to the fact that there do not appear to be as many social conventions. This is called the 'online dis-inhibition effect'.

This leaves trolls to feel they can pretty much say whatever they want to say without real-world consequences because of the physical and emotional disconnect of a computer screen.

While not all trolls remain anonymous, it is easy to take the route of anonymity on the internet, which provides an even greater distance between the troll and the person they are abusing online. This then gives them the freedom to act in whichever way they want in order to get a reaction online.

How to react and respond to trolls?

If you or your child are dealing with trolls, this can be tough and difficult. Your child's online space should be a safe one and they shouldn't have to feel scared or ashamed every time they log in to one of their accounts. Here are some ways to deal with trolls, should you or your child ever be targeted:

- Don't feed the troll. Generally, people who exhibit this type of behaviour online are wanting to gauge a reaction from the victim. If you choose not to react to the hateful comments, it is likely that the cyberbully will become bored and move on.

- Delete comments. If you find that someone has responded to content that you have posted in an offensive or negative way, make sure to delete the comment as soon as you see it. If it feels necessary, take a screenshot of it as well.

- Block the user who is sending you harmful stuff. If you ever feel attacked in any way by someone on the internet, block them. If a user is blocked, it is impossible for them to interact with you on your page with that particular account.

- Report the comments or responses to the app or website. If you report repulsive content on social media, it is likely that the comment, message or account reported will be suspended or even deactivated.

- Contact the police. 'Doxing' is a term which means to search for and publish private or identifying information about a particular individual on the Internet, typically with malicious intent. If this is the case for you, go to the police.

- Be aware of what you are putting up online. Try not to disclose any personal information about yourself, or things you would not want others to know or use against you.

How is this problem being solved?

While in the midst of being cyberbullied, it might feel as though it is impossible to escape. This is not the case. There are many things happening in order to ensure that social media is a safe and reliable space for you to go to in order to connect with your friends and family:

Social media channels:

Twitter, Youtube, Instagram, Facebook and Snapchat have made it easier to report abuse or hateful and offensive comments online. Their goal is to have their platform be a safe place for people to go to and share things in a secure way.

Authorities:

Home Secretary Amber Rudd has announced the online hate crime hub to tackle online hate crime. It will ensure better support for victims and help drive up the number of prosecutions.

This hub will be run by the police officers for National Police Chiefs Council (NPCC), and will work in order to enable these cases to be looked at and sorted effectively and efficiently.

Laws:

While some of the older laws regarding internet safety and protection are still in use, many believe that they need to be updated or new laws need to be put in place. Current laws are the Communications Act 2003 and the Obscene Publications Act 1959 and 1964.

What you can do:

Make sure you or your child deletes and reports negative or offensive activity on their page. Always seek advice and don't go through these things alone - if you are a parent, you can support your child. If you are a child - always approach a parent, carer, teacher or trusted adult.

26 July 2018

Fight against cyberbullying launched in Dundee

A new campaign to fight online bullying has been launched in Tayside.

By Emma Crichton

DigiKnow was unveiled at Dundee Science Centre on Tuesday as part of Safer Internet Day and has already been backed by some of the world's biggest IT companies.

The initiative will provide teachers with resources and support to use the internet for education, while teaching children to protect themselves from cyberbullying and exploitation.

DigiKnow was developed in a partnership between the Scottish Government, Police Scotland, a Young Scot steering group of teenagers, and Education Scotland, as part of the recently launched Digital Schools Awards programme. It has been backed by technology companies HP, Microsoft and Intel.

Maree Todd, Scotland's minister for children and young people, said: 'The proliferation of the internet and advances in digital technologies have brought around much positive change but in an age when mobile technologies are integrated into almost every aspect of our lives, ensuring young people enjoy a positive experience online needs to be a top priority.

'This is the first initiative of its kind to be delivered in Scotland and supports teachers with information and practical resources. By doing so we are better equipping them to educate pupils on the benefits and potential dangers of the internet.'

The launch comes as one in four children in Scotland aged between eight and 11 have their own social media profiles.

Schools can apply for an internet safety resilience badge by carrying out an assessment to find flaws in their knowledge. DigiKnow can then be used to fill any gaps and improve teachers' expertise.

George Brasher, managing director of HP UK and Ireland, said: 'Keeping young people safe online has never been more important.

'Through this initiative, HP is proud to support schools in ensuring young people grow up in a culture where staying safe online is as natural to them as any other aspect of their digital lives.'

6 February 2019

Building confidence after online bullying

Online bullying can really knock your confidence. But you can try taking control. You can build up your confidence and feel better about yourself. Find out how.

Getting your confidence back

Cyberbullying or bullying on social networks is upsetting and confusing. You might really struggle to feel confident afterwards. But we're here to help you build your confidence back up bit by bit.

You could try all of these ideas, or just the ones that sound right for you. You may have to find the right combination of things. So stick with it and keep trying our tips for feeling confident.

And often the more confident you feel, the more you can deal with bullying.

Seven ways to feel in control

1. Talk about what's going on

It might not always feel like talking will be useful. But it is. It can really help.

Talk about what's on your mind. Telling someone about what's happening helps you see your situation from a different perspective.

Think about who would be a good person to talk to. Normally the best listeners are people who you feel comfortable around.

You could talk to:

- a close friend
- an adult you trust
- a Childline counsellor.

You don't have to talk about everything. Just mentioning some of what's going on can really help.

2. Give up the guilt

You might think you've done something wrong or that you deserve online bullying. But this isn't true.

People who bully often do it because:

- they're jealous
- they want to feel powerful
- they're trying to hide something negative in their own lives like feeling bad about how they look or not having a happy home life.

If someone is spreading rumours about you online or posting hateful messages, it says more about them than about you. The bullying is not your fault, so don't feel guilty because you've done nothing wrong.

3. Use anger positively

If someone's bullying you online, it's completely normal to feel angry. Being angry is okay. Anger can stop you feeling defeated.

But always remember that anger isn't the same as aggression. Being angry doesn't mean posting an abusive message to the other person. Anger can become a problem if it makes you want to hurt someone, break something or hurt yourself.

Try to understand your anger. See what it looks like and draw what it feels like to be angry.

You can then use anger to make positive changes in your life. That might be joining our message boards. It could be finding a new place to go and make friends. Or, if you feel confident enough, you could use your anger to block or report someone who is sending you nasty comments. It's all about taking the anger from the bullying, and turning the energy into something positive.

4. Try new things

Trying something new is one of the best ways to rebuild your confidence. It could be anything – even little things, like eating lunch in a different place or putting your hand up in a lesson. You could try a new hobby or talk to someone you haven't spoken to before. It may seem hard at first, but doing new things often gets easier the more you try it.

You might think that you can't do something. But then when you try it, you find that actually you can do it. And that's how confidence happens.

If you find it hard to stop checking Facebook or Twitter for nasty messages, you could try something new on the internet for the first time.

Why not, play a game, start a new thread on our message boards or reply to a message which nobody has replied to yet? You could try writing a blog, article or short story for the first time – if you don't want people to know you wrote it, you could publish it anonymously, with no name next to it.

5. Let go of the nastiness

Anybody can experience bullying. If you're going through cyberbullying, it's not your fault. Don't blame yourself.

It's not always easy to let go of the blame though. Try thinking of the other person's (or people's) negativity as a hot potato. If they dump their nastiness on you, make sure you don't hold onto it. You could do this by writing down your thoughts, doing some drawing or going outside (without your phone) to do some exercise or go for a walk. It's all about finding a way to make sure the bad feelings don't weigh you down.

6. Express yourself

You could also use the Wall of Expression game. Write down how you feel and then smash it away. When you smash the wall or finish your drawing, try to think of it as letting go of the negativity.

You could also try getting a piece of paper and finishing this sentence: 'I feel…because….' Keep writing it as many times as you can. When you can't do it anymore, scrunch up the piece of paper and throw it away. Or you could keep it safe somewhere until you feel ready to throw it away. Remember, it's all about learning to control bad feelings and how to get rid of them. So do what feels right for you.

If you're getting nasty messages on your phone, you could release the negative feelings by texting someone to tell them how you feel.

7. Remember that difference is amazing

Being different is okay. We are all different. And that's a positive thing.

Someone might be making you feel bad by sending you messages about being different. But being different is an amazing thing. What if there was only one colour in the world? Or one sport? Or one type of music? Life would be very boring. So don't forget that our differences are important – they are what make you who you are.

Go on a cyber holiday

It can be difficult to take your mind off online bullying sometimes. This is natural.

But the problem with worrying about online bullying is that it gives you no time to relax and enjoy yourself. And this isn't healthy for you. It's really important to have time to be 'you' and not have to worry about it online.

You could go on a 'cyber holiday' where you don't go on any social networks for a set amount of time. It might be a few days or it could be a week. It's up to you. You could tell everyone that you won't be going online for a while. Or, if you prefer, you don't have to announce it. You can just take a break for a while. It might be difficult, but it could help break the cycle of bullying until you feel confident enough to go back on.

Why not set yourself a small goal? Like instead of refreshing your profile every five minutes try something you enjoy. Do whatever helps you feel on top.

Tips from other young people

- Take a screenshot of the bullying, so you can show it to an adult.

- Don't be afraid to be the one who speaks out if a joke goes too far.

- Block anyone who bullies you.

- Know your rights. Under Section 127 of the Communications Act 2-3, you can report anyone who is 'grossly offensive' or causes 'needless anxiety'. Find out how to block people on different social networks.

- Don't reply to a bullying status or message about you, it's what they want you to do!

- Report it to CEOP if the bullying involves a naked or topless image of you (or if people are trying to make you send these kinds of images), CEOP work with the police to help keep you safe online.

December 2017

Key Facts

- YoungMinds' *Safety Net Report* discovered almost 30% of young people spend more than four hours each day browsing social media, with 44% admitting to three or more hours per day. 61% admitted to creating their first social media account before the age of 12 (despite guidelines requiring users to be 13 or older). (page 1)

- 62% of young people reported that social media had impacted their friendships, with a further 38% saying it had a negative impact on how they feel about themselves. (page 1)

- Amost one in two (46%) of young women and girls found that social media had, and continued to negatively impact their self-esteem. (page 1)

- YoungMinds and The Children's Society spoke to over 1,000 young people aged 11–25 to get a greater idea of the scope of cyberbullying. Almost half (47%) reported an experience with threatening, intimidating or nasty messages through social media, email or text. (page 3)

- In the year ending March 2018, 7% of children said that they had experienced cyberbullying. (page 3)

- In the year ending March 2018, girls were more likely than boys to have experienced cyberbullying (9% compared to 5%). (page 4)

- Research reveals that you're more likely to be cyberbullied by a total stranger. Four in ten (44%) of those who've experienced it say it came from someone they'd never spoken to online or in person before. This is particularly common among those aged 55 and above (56%). (page 8)

- Just over half (53%) of those who've experienced cyberbullying have never reported the incident to the website or service in question. (page 9)

- A third (29%) of people who've experienced cyberbullying say they carried on with life as normal, with no particular consequences. (page 9)

- Most bullying is face-to-face – with cyberbullying used as a modern tool to supplement traditional forms. (page 10)

- 29% of UK teenagers reported being bullied – only 1% were victims of cyberbullying alone. (page 10)

- Disabled children and children with special needs report much higher incidents of bullying than other pupils. (page 11)

- DfE survey results showed that pupils who were victims of bullying received lower GCSE results than their peers who hadn't been bullied. (page 11)

- Researchers at Oxford, Swansea and Birmingham Universities found that cyberbullying raised the risk of self-harm or suicidal behaviour 2.3 times. (page 19)

- Bullies were also around 20 per cent more likely to have self-harmed or attempted suicide than non-bullies. (page 19)

- A recent study found that online bullying has grown by 88% in just five years. (page 20)

- The largest reported reason surrounding why people troll is due to the anonymity of the internet: put simply, they can get away with it more so than real life. (page 20)

- A recent YouGov poll found of the 1,003 secondary-age students surveyed, 39% said bullying had affected their grades, 38% said they had missed school because they were so frightened of bullies. More than a fifth (22%) said bullying had become so intense that they had been forced to change schools. (page 22)

- The UK introduced the world's first online safety laws in April 2019. Social media companies and tech firms are required to protect their users or face tough penalties if they do not comply. (page 24)

- Research consistently finds that cyberbullying is associated with a number of social, emotional and academic problems. Young people who are involved in cyberbullying, either as offender or victim, are also more likely to think about and attempt suicide. (page 28)

- About one in eight parents do not set any rules about what their children do online. (page 28)

- Children are less likely to cyberbully others when they believe that their parents are likely to punish them for such behaviour. (page 29)

- Legally, you have to be over 16 to use WhatsApp. (page 32)

- 'Grooming' is when adults pretend to be young people online and try to engage other young people in inappropriate activities. This is a criminal offence. (page 34)

- According to Kick It Out's study, there have been an estimated 134,400 discriminatory posts this 2017/18 season related to the Premier League alone. (page 34)

- 'Doxing' is a term which means to search for and publish private or identifying information about a particular individual on the Internet, typically with malicious intent. (page 36)

Glossary

Bullying

A form of aggressive behaviour used to intimidate someone. It can be inflicted both physically and mentally (psychologically).

Catfishing

A type of impersonation involving stealing someone's identity and posing as them to decieve others.

Cyberbullying

Cyberbullying is when technology is used to harass, embarrass or threaten to hurt someone. A lot is done through social networking sites such as Facebook and Twitter. Bullying via mobile phones is also a form of cyberbullying. With the use of technology on the rise, there are more and more incidents of cyberbullying.

Exclusion

Intentionally leaving someone out of a group, such as group messaging, online apps and gaming sites.

Flaming

Flaming involves using extremely offensive language in order to get into online arguments or fights.

Harassment

Usually persistent (but not always), a behaviour that is intended to cause distress and offence. It involves sending offensive, insulting or humiliating online comments or messages, or being offensive on gaming sites.

Non-verbal abuse

Can be thought of as a kind of 'psychological warfare' because instead of using spoken words or direct physical violent behaviour, this form of abuse involves the use of mimicry (teasing someone by mimicking them), offensive gestures or body language.

Racist bullying

Targeting a person because of their race, colour or beliefs. There is a difference between racism and racial harassment: racial harassment refers to words and actions that are intentionally said/done to make the target feel small and degraded due to their race or ethnicity.

Self-harm/self-injury

Self-harm is the act of deliberately injuring or mutilating oneself. People injure themselves in many different ways, including cutting, burning, poisoning or hitting parts of their body. Self-harmers often see harming as a coping strategy and give a variety of motivations for hurting themselves, including relieving stress or anxiety, focusing emotional pain and as a way of feeling in control. Although prevalent in young people, self-harm is found amongst patients of all ages. It is not usually an attempt to commit suicide, although people who self-harm are statistically more likely to take their own lives than those who don't.

Sexual bullying

This includes a range of behaviours such as sexualised name-calling and verbal abuse, mocking someone's sexual performance, ridiculing physical appearance, criticising sexual behaviour, spreading rumours about someone's sexuality or about sexual experiences they have had or not had, unwanted touching and physical assault. Sexual bullying is behaviour which is repeated over time and intends to victimise someone by using their gender, sexuality or sexual (in)experience to hurt them.

Social media

Media which are designed specifically for electronic communication. `Social networking' websites allow users to interact using instant messaging, share information, photos and videos, and ultimately create an online community. Examples include Facebook, Instagram, Twitter and WhatsApp.

Trolling

Trolling is when someone intentionally posts something online to provoke a reaction. The idea behind the trolling phenomenon is that it is about humour, mischief, and some argue, freedom of speech; it can be anything from a cheeky remark to a violent threat. However, sometimes these Internet pranks can be taken too far, such as a person who defaces an internet tribute site, causing the victim's family further grief.

Verbal abuse

Spoken words out loud intended to cause harm, such as suggestive remarks, jokes or name-calling.

Activities

Brainstorming

- In small groups, discuss what you know about cyberbullying:

  - Give some examples of cyberbullying.

  - Why do people engage in cyberbullying?

  - Who is affected by cyberbullying?

  - How does cyberbullying differ from other types of bullying? Why do you think this?

Research

- Create an anonymous questionnaire that will be distributed throughout your year group, to find out how many people have experience of cyberbullying. Decide whether you want to focus on people who have been cyberbullied, or people who are cyberbullies. Then work with a partner to construct at least ten questions. Distribute your questionnaire, thinking carefully about how people will return it anonymously, then gather your results and create a presentation for your class, including graphs and infographics if appropriate.

- Take a look at your school's anti-bullying policy and how it defines cyberbullying. Are there any additions you would make to the policy? Discuss with the class and write up suggested amendments to the policy.

- Use the Internet to research anti-bullying campaigns. Choose one you think is particularly effective and sends a strong message. Dicuss with a classmate.

- Speak to an adult you know about their experiences of childhood bullying. Ask them about how it affected them in the long-term, whether they were a victim, perpetrator or bystander.

Design

- In small groups, design a school-based campaign that will highlight the effects of cyberbullying. You should choose one particular type of cyberbullying for your campaign; for example: nasty text messages, impersonation, denigration, exclusion, sexting or trolling. You could use posters, articles in your school magazine, assemblies or even a website. Be creative!

- Imagine you work for a company that is experiencing problems with workplace bullying among its staff. Create an engaging email that will highlight the issue, including advice for anyone who is affected.

- Design a horizontal banner that could be displayed as an advert on websites to highlight the effects of cyberbullying.

- Choose one of the articles from this book and create an illustration that highlights the key themes of the piece.

- Create a meme with an anti-cyberbullying message.

Oral

- As a class, write down made-up cyberbullying scenarios on sticky notes (anonymously) and put them in a jar. Select a scenario at random and read it aloud or roleplay the situation and discuss appropriate ways to deal with each one.

- Discuss why some types of bullying might be more serious than others.

- In pairs, go through this book and discuss the cartoons you come across. Think about what the artists were trying to portray with each illustration.

- A friend uploads a comment on social media: *"Feeling upset... why won't people just leave me alone?"* Discuss how seeing this would make you feel and how you would respond to your friend.

Reading/writing

- Write a list of the reasons why bullying is so hard to tackle and why it is even harder to do so when the bullying is online.

- Imagine you have cyberbullied someone and now you realise and regret the suffering you have caused. Write a letter of apology to your victim explaining why you did it and why you are sorry.

- Write a list of the actions you can take to protect yourself from cyberbullying. For example: keeping your passwords secret and not posting personal information that can identify you in any way. What other steps can you take to stay safe online?

Index

Acknowledgements

The publisher is grateful for permission to reproduce the material in this book. While every care has been taken to trace and acknowledge copyright, the publisher tenders its apology for any accidental infringement or where copyright has proved untraceable. The publisher would be pleased to come to a suitable arrangement in any such case with the rightful owner.

Images

Cover image courtesy of iStock. All other images courtesy of Pixabay, rawpixel.com and Unsplash.

Illustrations

Don Hatcher: pages 13 & 33 Simon Kneebone: pages 16 & 36 Angelo Madrid: pages 1 & 21.

Additional acknowledgements

With thanks to the Independence team: Shelley Baldry, Danielle Lobban, Jackie Staines and Jan Sunderland.

Tracy Biram

Cambridge, September 2019